CW01474986

ROUGH PAST
MEETS
NEW DESIGN

The Deutsche Nationalbibliothek lists this publication in
the Deutsche Nationalbibliografie; detailed bibliographic
data are available on the Internet at http://dnb.dnb.de

ISBN 978-3-03768-220-3
© 2017 by Braun Publishing AG
www.braun-publishing.ch

The work is copyright protected. Any use outside of the
close boundaries of the copyright law, which has not
been granted permission by the publisher, is unautho-
rized and liable for prosecution. This especially applies
to duplications, translations, microfilming, and any
saving or processing in electronic systems.

1st edition 2017

Editor: Editorial Office van Uffelen
Editorial staff and layout: Vanessa Stängle, Celine Zaiser
Translation: Judith Vonberg
Graphic concept: Michaela Prinz, Berlin
Reproduction: Bild1Druck GmbH, Berlin

All of the information in this volume has been compiled
to the best of the editor's knowledge. It is based on the
information provided to the publisher by the architects'
and designers' offices and excludes any liability. The
publisher assumes no responsibility for its accuracy or
completeness as well as copyright discrepancies and
refers to the specified sources (architects' and designers' offices). All rights to the photographs are property of
the photographer (please refer to the picture credits).

ROUGH PAST
MEETS
NEW DESIGN

CHRIS VAN UFFELEN

BRAUN

CONTENT

LAYERS OF TIME

ROUGH RENAIS-SANCE

In 2001, the opening of the new "site de création contemporaine" in the Palais de Tokyo in Paris stunned practitioners of art and architecture around the world: Anne Lacaton and Jean-Philippe Vassal had completely gutted the building near the Trocadéro, entirely removing its core. The exhibition space was built by Dondel, Aubert, Viard and Dastugue for the 1937 Paris exposition in the monumental style of the time and had now been returned to a state similar to that of a building site. Interior partitions had been removed and the remaining walls stripped down to the bare concrete. And that was it. Construction fencing blocked off the entrance area, while the ticket office was housed in a wagon conventionally used on building sites. The architects did, of course, also stabilize the structurally vulnerable building, which had been neglected for decades; but as soon as the meager budget of three million euros had been depleted, they declared the work finished. And Paris has since been home to an exhibition space for contemporary art that reinstates the city as one of the world's greatest art metropolises in the world.

This particular esthetic of the unfinished, the run-down and the shoddily repaired state, was not new. It was alive in modernism in the sculptures of Auguste Rodin, who saw perfection in the unfinished works of Michelangelo and thus rediscovered the "non-finito,"

a concept that had played a significant role in Renaissance theories of art. Leonardo da Vinci saw in the abstraction of imperfect works one of the elements that gave the art of painting a higher value than that of sculpture. At the same time, architecture was also discovering the esthetic value of incompleteness in the form of ancient ruins. It is believed to be Donato Bramante who created the first man-made ruins featuring bare brickwork in the Nymphaeum in Genazzano at the start of the 16th century. Man-made ruins were especially popular during the 18th and 19th centuries as follies in landscaped parks; while in the world of painting, Robert Hubert prophesized the esthetic of artificial ruins long before Caspar David Friedrich used these as a motif. In the context of landscaped gardens, simple pastoral architectural forms and ostensibly time-worn structures were also introduced as esthetic components. The Hameau de la Reine is a prominent example of this; a rustic retreat, or farming village, built by Richard Mique for Marie Antoinette as an ornamental feature adjacent to the summer residence in the garden of the Palace of Versailles. The masonry has been left visible, the plastering is irregular and the beams are crooked. A farming family was of course acquired to perfect the romantic illusion of happy lives lived in harmony with nature.

Lacaton & Vassal: Palais de Tokyo, Paris, 2001

8
LAYERS OF TIME

RURAL
ROTTEN
ROMANTIC

This romantic appreciation of ruins and the rural ambience, of the imperfect, the broken, the antiquated and the worn-out state, still continues today and forms the basis for understanding and evaluating the creations presented in *Rough Past meets New Design*. In every project, a historical layer of architecture is the foundation for a new creation, just like in Carlo Scarpas' renovation of the Castelvecchio in Verona (1959 to 1973). His idiosyncratic Brutalist architectural language transformed ruins into museum-like, functional rooms while wholly preserving their original character. Even earlier, from 1952 to1957, Hans Döllgast repaired a bomb crater that had left a gaping hole in the middle of Leo von Klenzes' building at the Alte Pinakothek in Munich using just the simplest of materials to achieve a kind of "arte povera" esthetic, although the building's ornamental decoration has been left perfectly intact, so the renovation is left to represent imperfection, rather than the new. The contour of the crater – created neither by the first nor the second architect, but rather a legacy of the Second World War – remains.

The more than 70 buildings featured in *Rough Past meets New Design* have been selected due to their playful interaction with layers of architectural history, whether truly ancient or more modern. In each case, these form the canvas for new creations that either blend or

contrast with the existing layers, or indeed do both at the same time. In this process, it is not just an ensemble of two moments in time that emerges, but the time between these architectural interventions and indeed the entire history of the ruins, the structure, or the locality become part of the new creation. History itself has been preserved, nestled between the structure's oldest and most recent layers.

Carlo Scarpa: Conservation of Castelvecchio, 1973,
Verona, with Scaliger tomb
Donato Bramante: Nympheum, 1511, Genazzano
Robert Hubert: The Grand Gallery in ruins, oil/canvas,
1796, Louvre, Paris
Michelangelo: Atlas-Slave, marble, 1523, Galleria dell'
Accademia, Florence
Richard Mique: Pigeonnier, 1783, Versailles

10

ZWARTE SILO DEVENTER THE NETHER-LANDS

WENINK HOLTKAMP ARCHITECTEN 2015

Overall view of Zwarte Silo after conversion
Ground floor after conversion
View over water seen through a large new window

The Zwarte Silo, or Black Silo in English, is an iconic building that marks the start of the harbor area in Deventer. It is the ideal venue for large public functions and brings a sense of dynamism to the area. With the transformation, the architects aimed to reinforce the building's connection with the harbor and to give the former industrial structure a new purpose.

The designers tried to stay as close as possible to the authentic raw character of the building. Key interventions include the introduction of several doors and windows with slender steel frames that enhance the facility's connection with its neighborhood. A large nine-meter window has been integrated on the east side, providing stunning views over the harbor area and creating a sense of openness in the design. The original separation of the main silo and the two low brick volumes was retained, with one area accommodating further food stalls and a bar, while the other contains a multipurpose space used for events.

NOW: WENINK HOLTKAMP ARCHITECTEN RE-ESTABLISHED THE SILO AS A FOCAL POINT OF THE COMMUNITY. BOASTING AN AREA OF 760 SQUARE METERS, THE ORIGINAL STORAGE SPACE IS NOW MAINLY USED FOR CATERING, EVENTS AND RESTAURANTS.

PAST: THE ORIGINAL GRAIN STORAGE SPACE WITH A CLOSED, RAW CHARACTER WAS BUILT BY MAARTEN VAN HARTE IN 1924, WHEN A.J. LAMMERS USED THE BUILDING FOR INDUSTRIAL PURPOSES. BRICK AND CONCRETE WERE THE PRIMARY MATERIALS USED TO BUILD THE STORAGE FACILITY.

Wide opening on east side
New entrance on north side
South side after conversion
Interior of main silo

15

MAAGDEN-TOREN ZICHEM BELGIUM DE SMET VERMEULEN ARCHITECTEN STUDIO ROMA 2015

Interior view with concrete piers
Exterior view of old and new structure

The Maagdentoren is a partially collapsed, fourteenth-century donjon or keep. Reconstruction is virtually impossible because the historical documentation is lacking and the building material, a local ironstone, is no longer available. The aim of the restoration was instead to consolidate the ruin, prevent further deterioration and render the tower accessible as a viewing platform for the surrounding landscape. The restoration was based on structural logic: the meter-thick, crumbling walls needed to be capped while structural repairs would ensure stability. A path leads to an access bridge, covered to protect visitors from falling debris.

On the inside, concrete piers replace collapsed cross vaults; on the outside, a brick shell closes the cylinder. Brick-sized openings illuminate the new stairs without the need to perforate the elevations with new and stylistically disruptive modern windows. The final stair to the roof winds up in a spiral, built into the shaft discovered in the wall. The steel structure that raises the meter-thick wall coping above the crumbling wall, and that in silhouette restores the circle, generates a tempietto, the upper level of which serves as an observation post.

NOW: DE SMET VERMEULEN ARCHITECTEN AND STUDIO ROMA RE-ESTABLISHED THIS TOWER FOR VLAAMSE OVERHEID AND AGENTSCHAP ONROEREND EFGOED, AFTER A PARTIAL COLLAPSE IN 2006. NOW USED AS A LOOKOUT, 633 SQUARE METERS WERE TRANSFORMED WITH CONCRETE, GALVANIZED STEEL AND PERERSEN-KOLUMBA BRICK.

PAST: THE ORIGINAL BUILDING, USED AS RESIDENTIAL TOWER, PRISON AND STORAGE, WAS BUILT IN THE FOURTEENTH CENTURY BY REINER II VAN SCHOONVORST. HE USED THE LOCAL STONE FROM DIEST FOR THE CONSTRUCTION.

Rooftop from outside
On top of tower
Interior staircase
Section
Ceiling construction

19
PROJECT COLLINS HAMBURG GERMANY
PLY STUDIO
2014

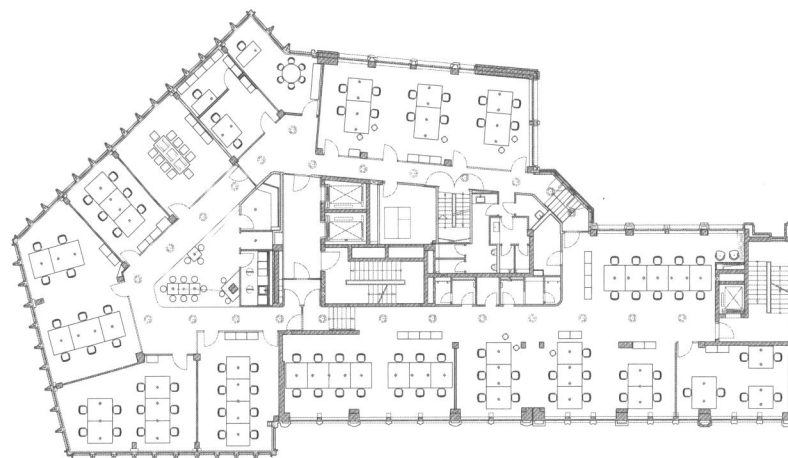

Seating area
Open space office
Master plan of open space office and tea kitchen

PLY designed and implemented this open space concept for up to 250 employees in line with existing regulations. The functional spatial planning, lighting concept and interior design elements were all tailored to suit the needs of the start-up that would make this office its home. The layout was in part determined by the unique architectural qualities of the existing building. Three building sections of varying construction types and ages were brought into dialogue with each other, both functionally and visually.

Diagonal concrete shafts in one building and historic brick façades in the original structure formed the outer layer, within which the home of Project Collins was developed. PLY's concept is based on an inter-action of surfaces. The old sand-blasted concrete surfaces find their antithesis in the coarsely meshed carpet, while open-pore woods lend warmth to the functional environment. The result combines clear functionality with a lighting and color concept that makes this space almost homely.

NOW: PLY STUDIO DEVELOPED THE ROOMS FOR PROJECT COLLINS AS AN OFFICE FOR AN ONLINE CLOTHING STORE. WITH AN AREA OF 3,000 SQUARE METERS, THE MAIN MATERIALS USED INCLUDED TEXTILES, WOOD AND CHALKBOARD COATING.

PAST: THE ORIGINAL COUNTING HOUSE, WITH A BRICK FAÇADE, WAS BUILT BY FREJTAG & ELINGIUS IN 1911 AND WAS MODIFIED IN THE 1980S.

Worktable in front of partition
Long office desk with Kandem 831 lamps by PLY
Workstation
Tea kitchen

22

THE APOLLO
GINZA
TOKYO
JAPAN
GEORGE
LIVISSIANIS
2016

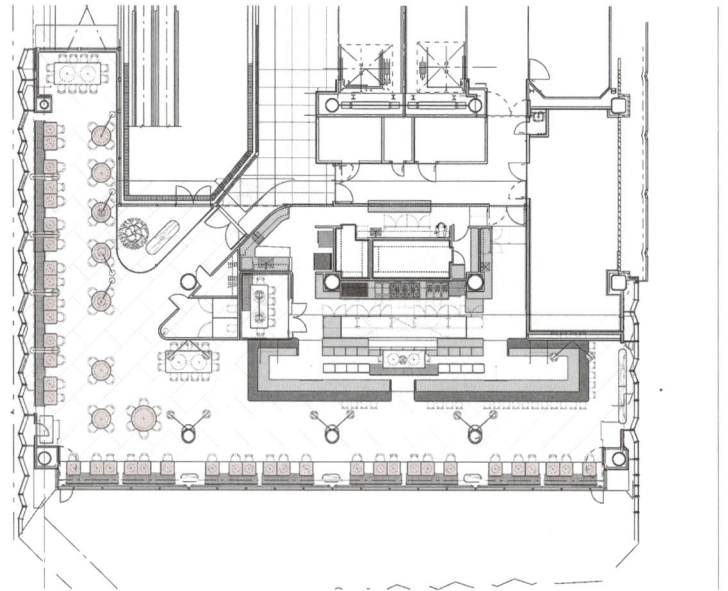

Raw concrete elements remind of harsh Greek landscape
General arrangement plan
Gray and white marble reminds of Greek culture

The simplicity of the space is generated by the balance of rawness and refinement exuded by the dusty color palette. The palette was chosen instead of the predictable combination of blue and white and visually echoes the rocky Greek island landscape.

The finishes are simple, naked and de-saturated of color. The intent was to expose the carcass of the building. A second layer of compressed cement sheeting serves to introduce new elements to the space, its curved corners adding fluidity and softness to the dining room. In this space, the furniture was selected and designed to generate a sense of lightness; the banquettes are free-standing and a soft palette was used in the finish of the bentwood chairs – a hand-applied soap finish that leaves them as true to their raw state as possible. The curtains balance the roughness of the original ceiling and walls, while the light quality from the parchment lampshades renders the space with a sense of calm and warmth. A subtle highlight of neon pink pays homage to the extensive use of the color red in Greek imagery.

NOW: THE ARCHITECT DESIGNED THIS MODERN GREEK RESTAURANT. BOASTING A FLOOR AREA OF 460 SQUARE METERS, COMPRESSED CONCRETE SHEETING, TERRAZZO, STEEL, MARBLE AND TEXTURED CEMENT RENDER WERE THE MAIN MATERIALS FOR THE CONSTRUCTION.

PAST: TOKYU PLAZA GINZA, AN 11-STORY RETAIL SPACE WITH GLASS FAÇADE, WAS BUILT BY NIKKEN SEKKEI LTD IN 2016. THIS BUILDING WAS ERECTED FOR TOKYU LAND CORPORATION IN THE MOST RENOWNED COMMERCIAL AND ENTERTAINMENT DISTRICT IN JAPAN.

View of the urban landscape
Elegant and lightweight furniture in brown tones
The kitchen with the same color palette
Brown tabletops and textile

27
THE COMMUNE SOCIAL SHANGHAI CHINA NERI&HU 2013

Bar in front of show kitchen
Exterior view

The Commune Social located at the Design Republic Design Commune in the center of Shanghai is a new tapas restaurant designed by Neri&Hu Design and Research Office. The food concept is a fresh and modern take on Spanish tapas. The design concept of the space was to emphasize the sharing idea of eating tapas in four distinct areas in the restaurant, tapas bar, dining room, dessert bar, and the secret bar.

First, gently removing the decaying wood and plaster, then carefully restoring the still vibrant red brickwork, while grafting on skin, joints, and organs onto parts that needed reconstruction, the designers breathed new life into a traditional colonial building plan. Neri&Hu strategically removed certain floor plates, walls and ceiling panels to allow a renewed experience of the existing building, one that is fitting for the new functions to which the building now needs to respond. The clear intentionality behind the detailing of connections between the old and the new lends a visually and spatially dynamic quality to the building as a whole.

NOW: NERI&HU RE-WORKED THE ORIGINAL BUILDING INTO A TAPAS RESTAURANT WITH A DISTINCTIVE CHARACTER. STRETCHING OVER 295 SQUARE METERS, RAW IRON, RECLAIMED WOOD, UNFINISHED CONCRETE AND EXPOSED BRICKS STILL CHARACTERIZE THE BUILDING.

PAST: THE ORIGINAL POLICE HEADQUARTERS WITH A CLOSED AND RAW CHARACTER WAS BUILT BY THE BRITISH IN THE 1920S.

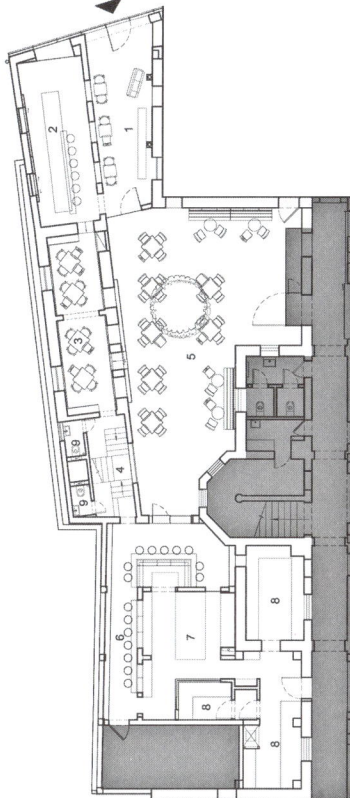

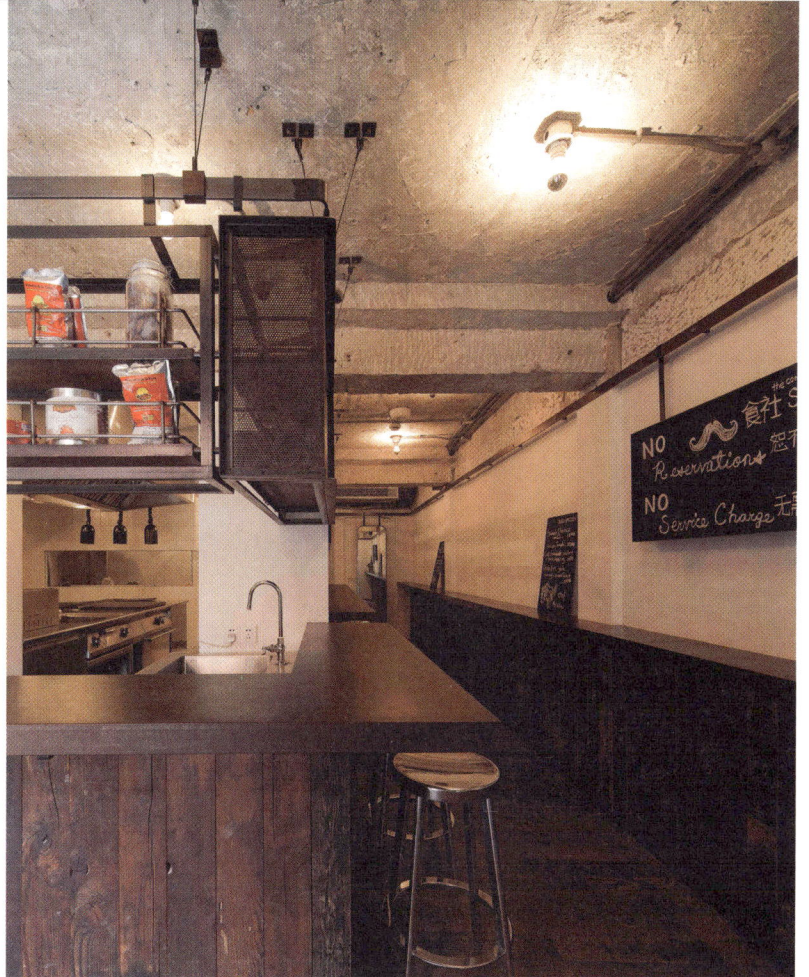

Dining room
Dessert bar
Ground floor plan
Way to tapas bar

31

STONE HOUSE SCAIANO SWITZERLAND

WESPI
DE MEURON
ROMEO
ARCHITECTS
2014

Exterior view
Kitchen and living room

The original house in the center of Scaiano comprised a main building, a vaulted cellar and two further stories. There was also an extension that was added later. The whole complex was characterized by the massive natural stone masonry. For more than two decades the house was uninhabited and an intensive redevelopment was therefore required to create a modern living environment with the appropriate insulation and other features. Nevertheless, the focus was to preserve the stone masonry, only replacing the wooden floor with new concrete floor. A new pitched roof was created on one side; and an accessible roof terrace on the other.

The main aim was to give the building a new charisma while maintaining the authentic façade that makes the building unique. The architects remodeled the old cellar into a main entrance. The bedrooms and the living area were transformed by glass fronts into modern light rooms. Throughout the project, the designers sought to create a new ensemble that did not jar with the original elements but rather complemented them.

NOW: THE RENOVATION WAS UNDERTAKEN BY WESPI DE MEURON ROMEO ARCHITECTS IN 2014. WITH AN AREA OF 183 SQUARE METERS, THE HOUSE WAS TRANSFORMED USING CONCRETE, GLASS AND WOOD.

PAST: THIS HOUSE IN SWITZERLAND COMPRISES MAINLY COBBLESTONE AND WOOD, AND WAS USED AS A DWELLING. THE BUILDING IS CHARACTERIZED BY ITS ARCHAIC SIMPLICITY.

Wardrobe
Kitchen
Entrance hall
Section
Bedroom

34

A. BAKER
CANBERRA
AUSTRALIA
DESIGNOFFICE
2013

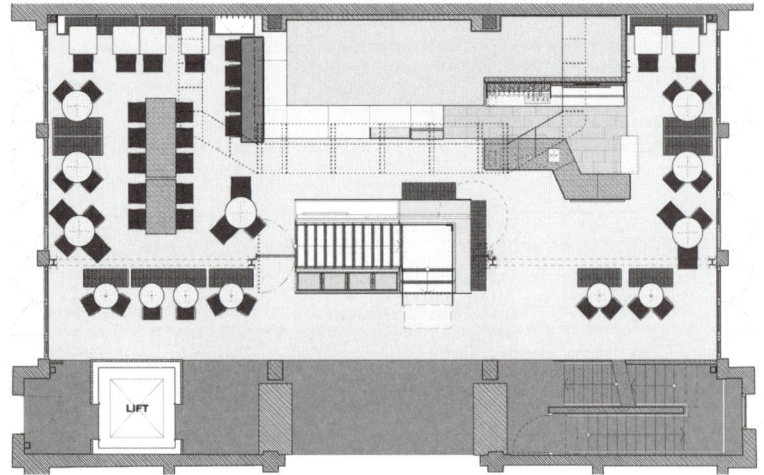

Ground floor dining room
Ground floor plan
Ground floor dining south

A. Baker is a bakery, bar, café and restaurant located in Canberra's New Acton precinct. Rising from the charred shell of the original building, it is a confident and contemporary juxtaposition of old and new. After the New Acton Pavilion was ravaged by fire in 2011, A. Baker occupied the charred shell of the ground floor and extended it into a newly formed basement.

On the ground floor, the history etched into the charred walls has been retained and embraced providing a textured and layered backdrop against the new palette of concrete, bluestone, galvanized steel and leather. The central open kitchen flanks the new staircase, providing controlled glimpses down to the A. Baker Speakeasy in the basement. The bar-room undercroft is anchored by a monolithic sculptural rolled steel bar and canopy, suspended in tension and lined in red Alicante marble. Cast-concrete seats and leather upholstery line the perimeter to provide an intimate venue with glimpses through into the working bakery next door and dining room above.

NOW: DESIGNOFFICE REMODELED THIS BUILDING INTO A RESTAURANT, BAR AND BAKERY. A LOVELY, WARM ATMOSPHERE WAS CREATED WITHIN THE 282-SQUARE-METER SHELL USING TIMBER, PAINTED STEEL, BLUESTONE, RED MARBLE AND TERRAZZO.

PAST: THE ORIGINAL HOTEL, BUILT FOR PUBLIC SERVANTS AND TOURISTS, WAS DESIGNED BY JOHN SMITH MURDOCH IN 1927. THE ORIGINAL BUILDING WAS CONSTRUCTED WITH BRICK WALLS AND A TIMBER FRAMED ROOF.

Detail of bluestone seating blocks
Basement bar
Stairs to basement bar
Ground floor dining area

39

ONDER DE LEIDING-STRAAT EINDHOVEN THE NETHER-LANDS MARJAN SARAB ARCHI-TECTURE 2014

Supermarket and entrance
Cash desk and seating area

Onder de Leidingstraat is located on the ground floor of an old Philips radio and television factory building in Eindhoven. The café, restaurant, deli and supermarket with organic products has been given a raw industrial and modern interior. The idea behind Onder de Leidingstraat was to create a place ideal for advertising and selling organic products with a homemade feel.

The kitchen is located in the center of the restaurant, allowing consumers to watch as their food is prepared. The height of the bar varies in order to create a unique experience for both the cooks and consumers depending on their position in the space. The central kitchen also establishes a border for the supermarket. Opposite the bar, the sitting space is arranged to optimize the use of sunlight and allows for different activities including eating, working and simply relaxing. Most of the materials on the floor and walls remain untouched, allowing the industrial character of the building to be preserved. The rest of the space has been kept simple and white while the furniture and plants are used to add color and variety.

NOW: MARJAN SARAB ARCHITECTURE TRANSFORMED A PART OF THE OLD BUILDING INTO A CAFÉ AND DELI. WITH A FLOOR AREA OF 163 SQUARE METERS, THE ORIGINAL PRODUCTION HALL HAS BEEN NOW REDESIGNED INTO A COZY PLACE TO RELAX AND EAT.

PAST: THE ORIGINAL PHILIPS RADIO AND TELEVISION FACTORY BUILDING WAS CONSTRUCTED IN 1928. THE BUILDING COMPRISED PRIMARILY CONCRETE AND METAL.

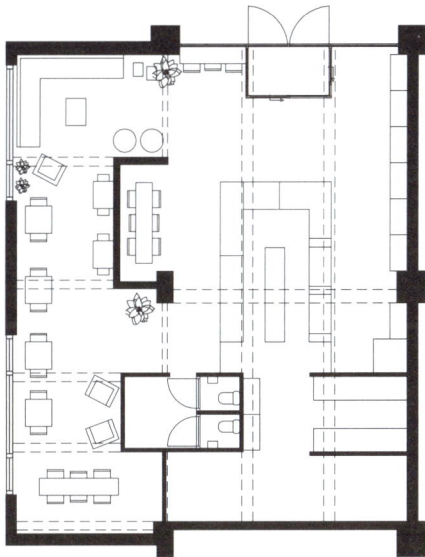

Seating area
Entrance
Detail with rough wall
Ground floor plan
Lounge area

43

BANKARA
SAITAMA
JAPAN

STUDIO201-ARCHITECTS
2014

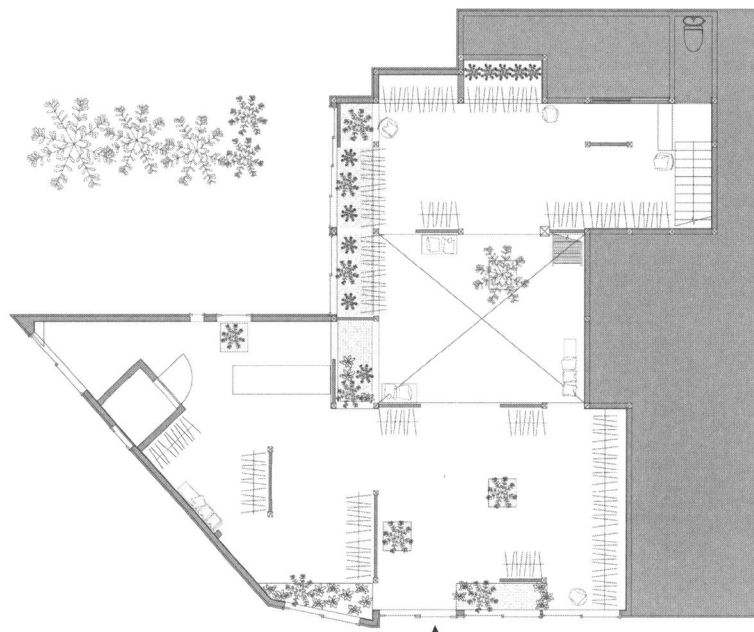

Interior view
First floor plan

The Bankara project involved the renovation of the ground floor of a house from the 1940s, transforming it into a vintage clothing store. It is characterized by a wooden roof construction that is rare among examples of modern architecture. By prioritizing the flow of natural light through different openings into the interior, the architect sought to draw attention to the most interesting aspects of the old house.

A three-meter tall maple is one of several trees that were planted as symbols of the building's relationship with nature. Additionally, plywood panels were installed between the pillars to create flow lines inside the store. The surrounding interior walls were painted white to accentuate and valorize the wooden structures. The concept of change and transformation was at the heart of the design: light flowing into the space at different times of day generates different moods, while the structural materials age over time, the growing trees and the changing clothes on display allow for seasonal and long-term developments. The aim was to create a space that reacts to the passage of time while exuding a charm that is timeless.

NOW: STUDIO201ARCHITECTS REMODELED THE OLD WOODEN HOUSE INTO A VINTAGE CLOTHING STORE. THE RENOVATION INCLUDED THE INTEGRATION OF OSB PANELS AND NEW WINDOWS AS WELL AS THE PLANTING OF SEVERAL TREES.

PAST: THE ORIGINAL RESIDENTIAL HOUSE WAS BUILT IN THE 1940S. THE HOUSE WAS LARGELY MADE OF WOOD AND WAS A CLOSED RATHER THAN AN OPEN STRUCTURE.

Different room sections
Showroom area
Exhibition space
Center of building

ART LOFT CHAI WAN HONG KONG CHINA MASS OPERATIONS 2014

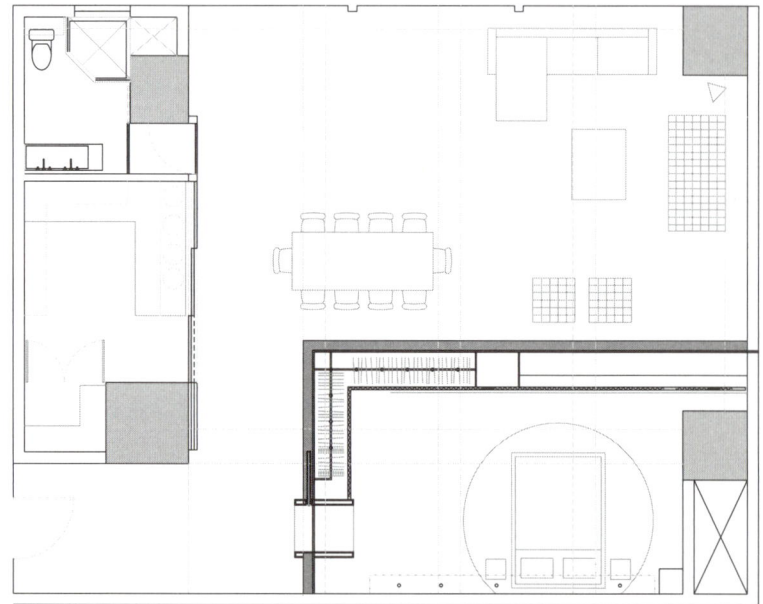

Floor plan level 8
Living area
Design elements in the loft

In a city that commands some of the highest rates per square meter rates for mostly underwhelming properties, industrial conversions are a popular and a budget-friendly option. The Art Loft in Chai Wan is Mass Operations' second loft in Hong Kong. Both are located in industrial zones and driven by an intention to generate better spaces than those available in the city's residential neighborhoods.

The owner of the Chai Wan Loft is an art collector; as such, his wish was to be able to display his art and book collection while also being able to entertain guests with views of the city. Opening and closing elements are used to hide and reveal spaces. The kitchen can be opened or closed by large sliding partitions creating a dynamic public living space. A general approach of industrial roughness and adhoc strategies were used to maintain the quality of the converted space; scraped beams and columns reveal the structural concrete, while exposed piping and machinery show the sense of urgency and perhaps temporality of the occupation of the space.

NOW: MASS OPERATIONS RENEWED AN APARTMENT IN CORNELL CENTER FOR AN ART COLLECTOR AS A COMFORTABLE AND SPACIOUS LIVING ENVIRONMENT. THE APARTMENT HAS 220 SQUARE METERS AND IS DIVIDED INTO LIVING AREA, KITCHEN AND BEDROOM.

PAST: THE ORIGINAL BUILDING WITH RAW CHARACTER WAS BUILT IN THE LATE 1970S AND WAS USED AS AN INDUSTRIAL WAREHOUSE STORAGE.

Exhibition space
Living area
Bathroom
View into living area

51

ABBOTSFORD WAREHOUSE APARTMENTS MELBOURNE AUSTRALIA ITN ARCHITECTS 2012

Living room
Balcony deck
Entry lounge and stairs

Designed by Nigel Grigg and Alexandra Neumann of ITN Architects, this former industrial warehouse has been converted into two three-story warehouse apartments by removing the roof, retaining the lower floors and constructing a new upper floor which has been set back on all sides to create upper decks and balconies.

Many of the old building's simple details were retained as well as the external walls and lower floors. New elements and materials sit side by side with the old to create contemporary apartments with old world charm. Old timber workshop welding benches were retained and used for the kitchen island benches with new in situ concrete bench tops added. New columns penetrate the island benches. Four-meter-high windows were converted into steel and glass front doors and electric garage doors to create an overwhelming effect upon entry, and match the scale of the existing four-meter-high ceilings. The old timber columns were removed, repaired and reinstated with concealed steel columns adjacent for strength. New services such as copper gas pipes and electrical conduits were exposed where suitable and left in their natural state.

NOW: ITN ARCHITECTS RE-ESTABLISHED THESE TWO WAREHOUSE APARTMENTS FOR ALEXANDRA NEUMANN BY USING STEEL, TIMBER, GLASS, CONCRETE AND CEMENT SHEETS. BOASTING AN AREA OF 600 SQUARE METERS, THE FORMER WAREHOUSE AND FACTORY IS NOW PRIMARILY USED AS LIVING SPACE.

PAST: THE ORIGINAL WAREHOUSE AND FACTORY WAS BUILT IN 1910. BRICK WAS THE MAIN MATERIAL USED IN THE CONSTRUCTION PROCESS.

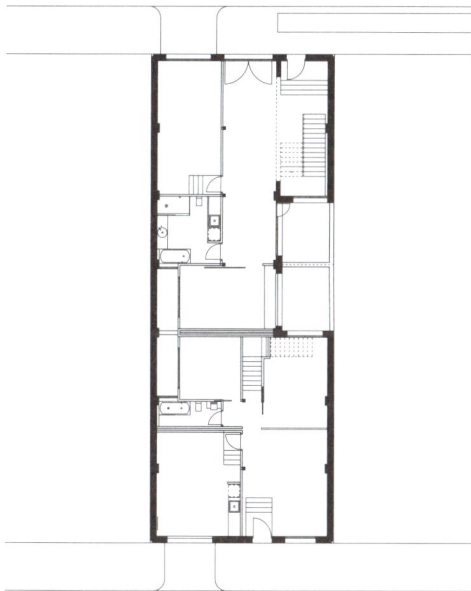

Bedroom and balcony
Living room and deck
Office
Ground floor plan
External façade

THE FUNK ZONE SANTA BARBARA CA, USA AB DESIGN STUDIO 2013

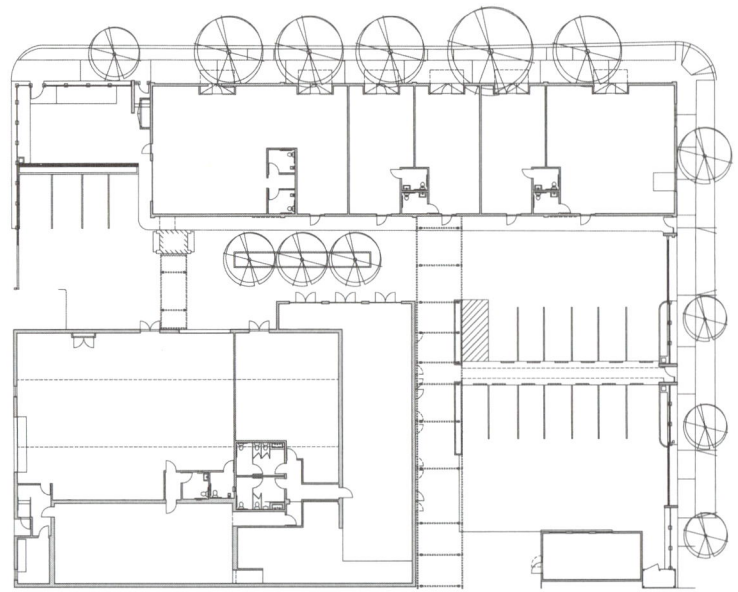

Site plan
Visitors and locals flock to a once-derelict area
Winery uses reclaimed barrels for display

The Funk Zone brings renewed life to an all-but-abandoned area of Santa Barbara's Waterfront District. AB Design Studio converted a rundown block into a center for food, wine, community and relaxation on a $3.6 million budget. The existing fish warehouse and processing buildings were reconceived into three separate buildings with new parking areas, courtyards, and landscape.

The old brick warehouse was maintained and repurposed to house new restaurants and bars, as well as both an active wine maker and craft beer brewery. The smaller building was converted into a take-out restaurant. Raw, galvanized, and corten steel, corrugated roofing and siding, and large roll-up doors maintain the industrial vibe. Individual establishments creatively incorporate reuse: all tables at The Lark restaurant are made from a single tree; Lucky Penny's façade comprises more than 15,000 actual pennies; furniture at Avelina Wine Production uses reclaimed-wood barrels; and Guitar Bar repurposes guitar-making Koa wood scraps as wall covering.

NOW: AB DESIGN STUDIO RE-ESTABLISHED THE OLD BUILDING FOR THE CENTRAL COAST REAL ESTATE AS A RESTAURANT AND RETAIL COMPLEX. MAINLY RAW, GALVANIZED AND CORTEN STEEL WAS USED TO CREATE A NEW ATMOSPHERE.

PAST: THE ORIGINAL FISH-PROCESSING WAREHOUSE AND FACTORY WAS BUILT WITH WOOD, PLASTER AND CONCRETE BLOCKS.

More than 15,000 pennies grace the façade
Former fish cold storage room is now a hip café
All restaurant tables are made from the same, single tree
Wood guitar-making scraps highlight the walls

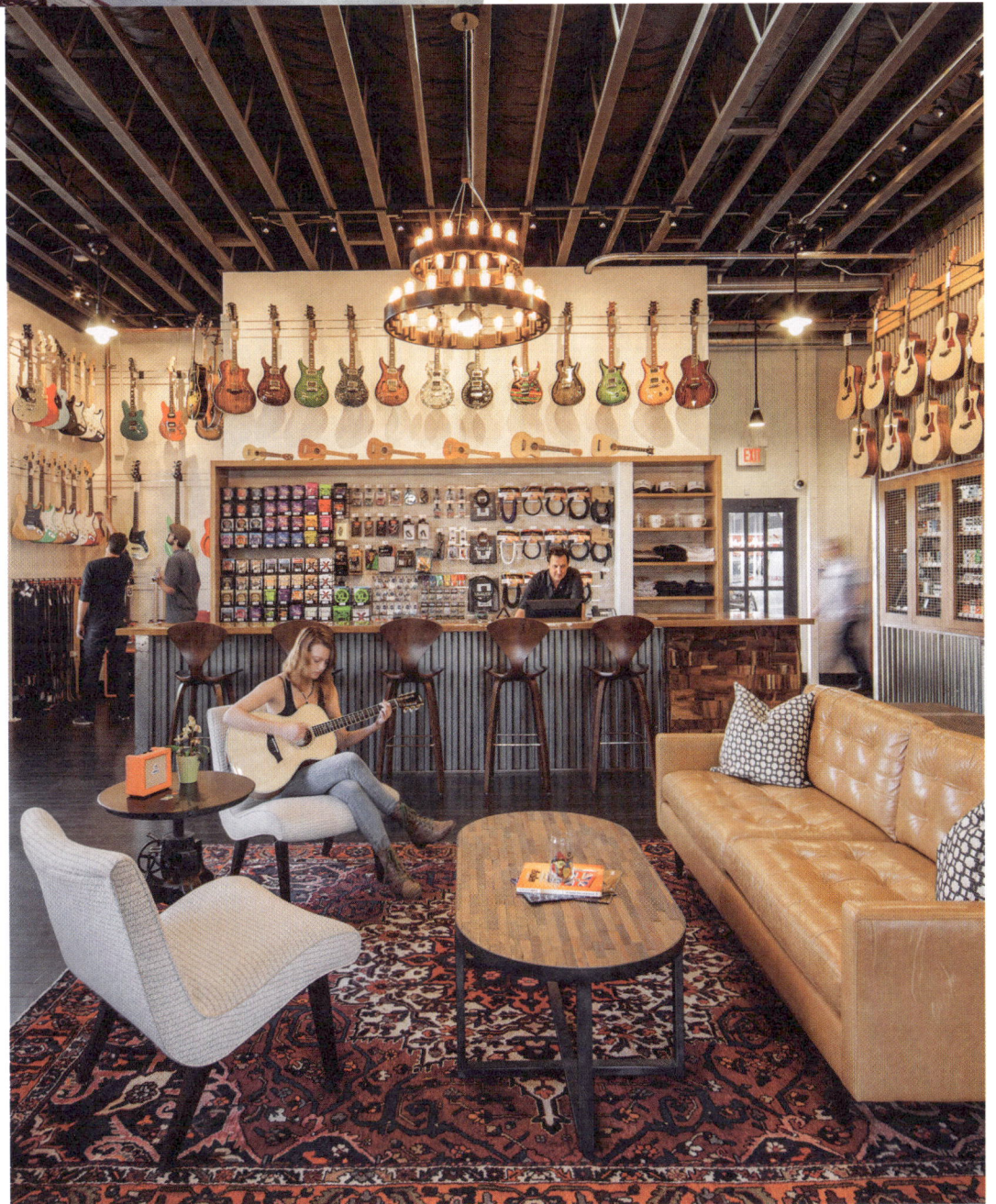

58

DOEHLER
NEW YORK
CITY
NY, USA
SABO
PROJECT
2014

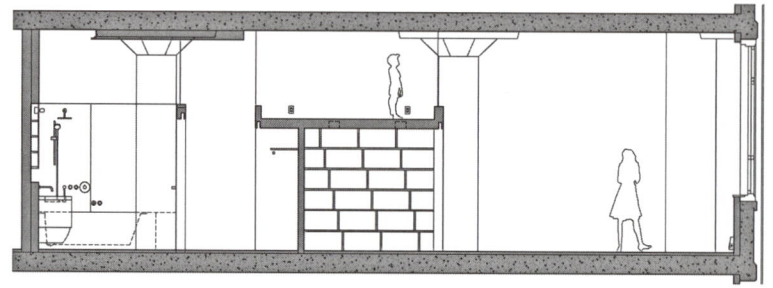

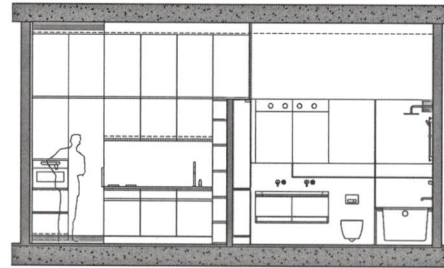

Sections
Kitchen with rough columns
Kitchen, mezzanine and workstation

Doehler involved the renovation of a Brooklyn loft located in a former die-casting factory built in 1913. After a 1980s residential conversion, all concrete columns and ceilings were concealed. The removal of most partitions and a vast dropped ceiling presented the opportunity to reveal the authenticity of the building as well as dramatically expanding the space.

Under the reclaimed ceiling, a new esthetic is defined by the height of a series of new partitions, custom cabinets, walk-in closet, glass enclosures and a new mezzanine. The vertical combination of opacities and transparencies manages privacy while bringing natural light to each space. The new connections between rooms establishes a continuum that seems to expand each space. A collection of wood containers stretches from the kitchen to the bedrooms while integrating stairs, display shelving, lighting and home office. The bathroom was designed around diamond shaped ceramic tiles. Different colors and shades have been combined in bold graphic patterns and gradients that wrap seamlessly around the walls and floor, seeming to flood the space with vibrant color.

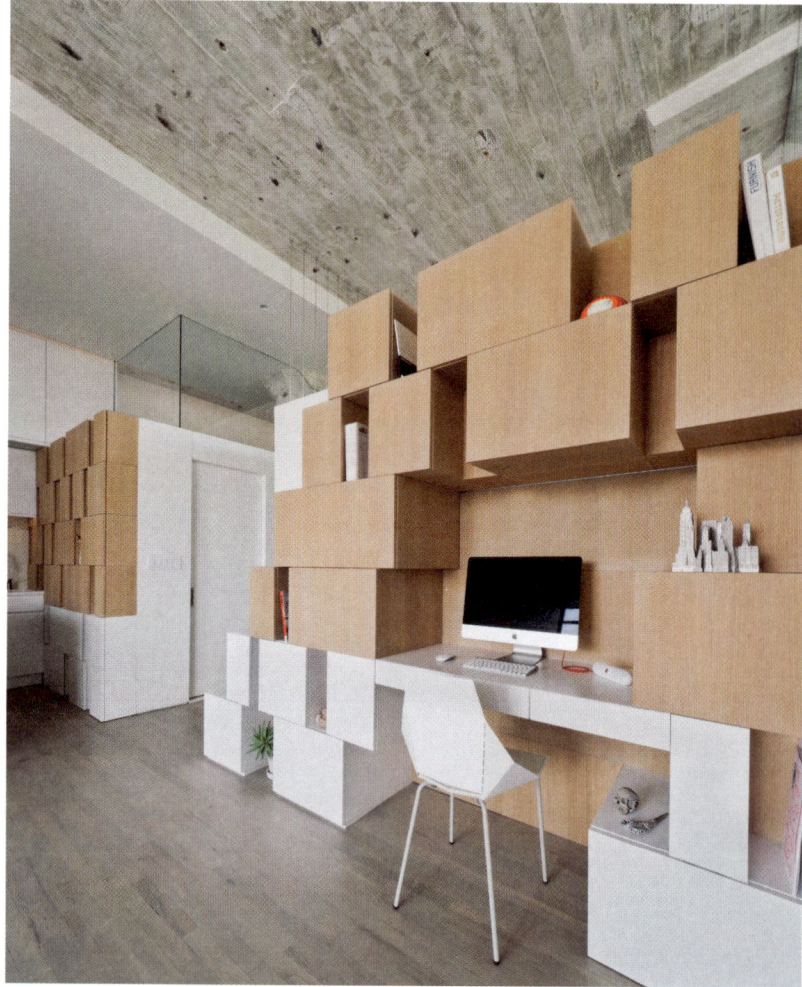

NOW: SABO PROJECT RENOVATED THIS 124-SQUARE-METER APARTMENT IN BROOKLYN FOR A PRIVATE CLIENT. THE URBAN FLAT WAS DESIGNED BY USING ROUGH CONCRETE, WHITE OAK, CERAMIC TILES, CALACATTA MARBLE AND BRUSHED NICKEL.

PAST: THE ORIGINAL DIE-CASTING FACTORY WAS BUILT IN 1913. IN THE 1980S IT WAS CONVERTED INTO A RESIDENTIAL BUILDING AND ALL THE CONCRETE COLUMNS AND CEILINGS WERE CONCEALED.

Stairs to mezzanine
Workstation with modern design
Bathroom
Rough column in bathroom

63

HOUSE OF VANS LONDON ENGLAND

BLACK SPARROW PRESENTS

TIM GREATREX ARCHITECTS HELLICAR STUDIO

2014

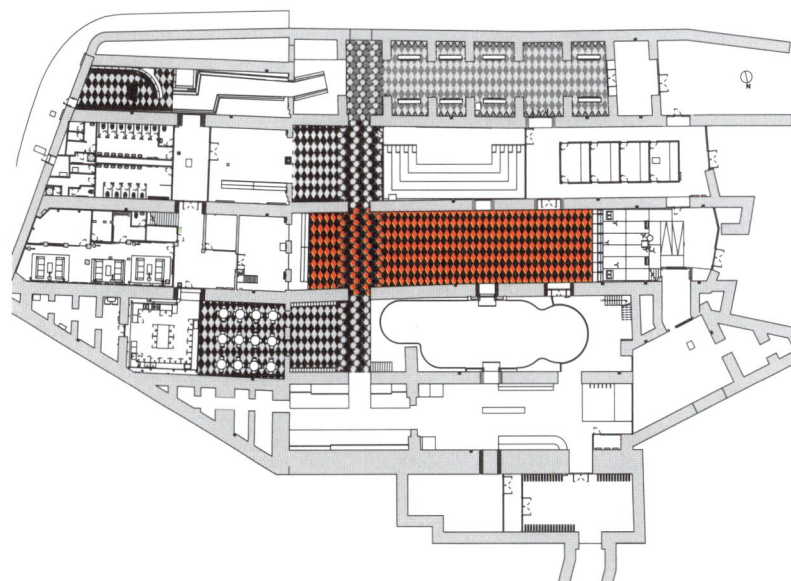

Rubber floor inspired by pattern of Vans shoe soles
Bar with painting by artist Mr. Penfold
Ground floor plan
Façade with historic arches

The House of Vans London is a mixed-use community space for London creative minds and those interested in skateboarding culture. It was established as a place to participate in the cultural lineage of skateboarding that has defined the Vans brand since 1966, combining skateboarding, art, film and music. The site is delineated into these four main activities so that each is housed within a specific tunnel. The venue, which opened in 2014, includes an art gallery, workshops, creative studio space, cinema, live music venue for 850 people, premium café, numerous bars and an indoor concrete skate park.

The freeholder does not allow any structural works or fixtures on the brickwork of the arches, not only to ensure the structural integrity of the supporting arches for the railway lines, but also to preserve the historic brickwork. The design represents an evolution of layered materials from the rawness of the existing brickwork tunnels through to the fit-for-purpose, clean palette of materials to create the café, bar, cinema, gallery space and gig venue.

NOW: BLACK SPARROW PRESENTS MANAGED THE CREATION OF THE 3,000-SQUARE-METER VENUE ACROSS FIVE TUNNEL SPACES IN CONJUNCTION WITH TIM GREATREX ARCHITECTS AND HELLICAR STUDIO WHO DESIGNED THE GALLERY, CINEMA, WORKSHOPS, GIG VENUE AND CAFÉ. THE SKATE PARK WAS DESIGNED BY MARC CHURCHILL AND GRAVITY SKATEPARKS.

PAST: THE 150-YEAR-OLD BRICK ARCHES, OWNED BY NETWORK RAIL, ARE SITUATED BELOW THE RAILWAY LINES HEADING OUT OF WATERLOO STATION, LONDON, NEXT TO THE FAMOUS GRAFFITI STREET, LEAKE STREET.

Concrete installations with gap to historic brickwork
The stage and gig tunnel
Downhill with outdoor metal-halide flood lighting
Rob Smith wallride
Kris Vile wallride

67

MERCAT AMSTERDAM THE NETHER-LANDS CONCRETE ARCHI-TECTURAL ASSOCIATES 2012

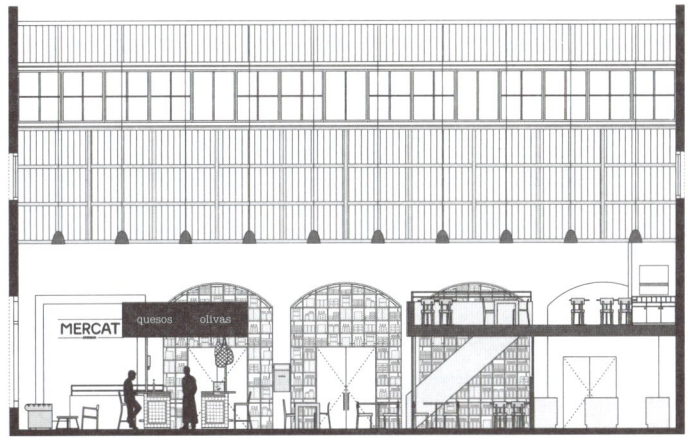

Industrial suspended lights in front of historic wall
Section
Exterior façade and summer terrace

Mercat is located in the up-and-coming eastern harbor area of the city, a place where visitors come to eat, drink and enjoy the surroundings. The building's exterior symbolizes the industrial heritage of Amsterdam, while the interior offers visual echoes of the raw characteristics of a Spanish market hall. The front and back façades, with their circular windows, original wooden gabled roof with its steel trusses, vertical skylights and brickwork walls with plastered decorations, lend character to the structure.

A market hall comes to life through the many stalls presenting numerous fresh products. The stalls in this space feature a slim, raw steel construction. The colorful signage typical for market stalls is abstracted to neon lettering. A wide variety of new and second-hand chairs symbolize the diversity and chaos of Spanish market halls. The selected Spanish products presented in three open cabinets enhance the market feeling with its organized chaos. By using clear shapes, grids and high contrast black-and-white images, a distinct graphic identity is created.

NOW: CONCRETE ARCHITECTURAL ASSOCIATES RE-ESTABLISHED THE BUILDING AS A RESTAURANT. WITH A FLOOR AREA OF 320 SQUARE METERS, THE ORIGINAL HARBOR AUTHORITY BUILDING IS NOW MAINLY USED FOR EATING AND DRINKING.

PAST: THE HARBOR POWER STATION WAS BUILT BY BASTIAAN DE GREEF AND WILLEM SPRINGER IN AN ECLECTIC STYLE IN 1885. THE FAÇADE IS EXECUTED IN RED BRICK WITH ALTERNATING BANDS OF NATURAL STONE. INSIDE, THE BUILDING HAS AN EXPOSED ROOF STRUCTURE WITH STEEL POLONCEAU TRUSSES. IT WAS RENOVATED IN 2001.

Original wooden gabled roof showing steel trusses
Neon letters above freestanding stall
Freestanding bar invites guests to sit down for a drink
Restaurant tables and cabinets close to freestanding stall

71

FOLSOM STREET LAB SAN FRANCISCO CA, USA
TODD VERWERS ARCHITECTS
2003

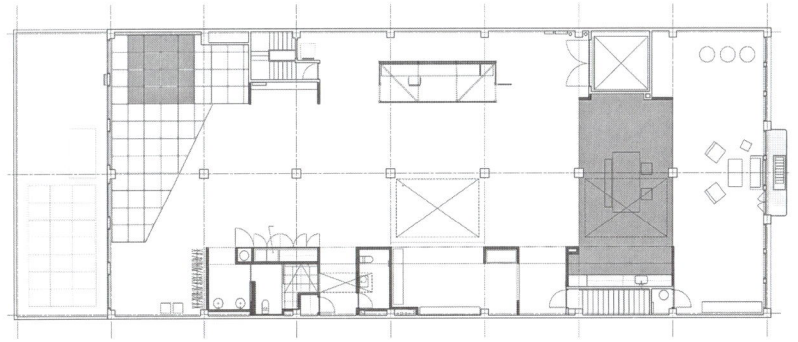

View through dining area to living room
Lounge and sleeping area
Floor plan of loft space
View into bathroom

Folsom Street Residential Laboratory is an urban loft space for a single resident and occupies the entire top floor in San Francisco's Soma neighborhood. The client's lifestyle is eclectic, blending professional, technology-based investigations with private activities and domestic functions.

The design draws heavily on the client's desire for a space exuding practical, modern simplicity. The space, essentially a toolbox for the owner's modern, urban lifestyle, is unique in its adaptation of commercial and institutional materials and components as residential functions. The kitchen is comprised of off-the-shelf laboratory cabinet modules, while a customized computer floor forms the sleeping platform, and a precision aluminum framing system creates the enclosure and adaptable framework for an "electronics laboratory." In some cases, these modular components were customized based on specific client requirements. The design was also heavily influenced by the client's sensitivities regarding esthetics, adaptability and re-use, prefabrication and modularity of components.

NOW: TODD VERWERS ARCHITECTS RENOVATED THE BUILDING BY USING GYPSUM, PHENOLIC RESIN AND OTHER MATERIALS. WITH AN AREA OF 550 SQUARE METERS, THE ORIGINAL FACTORY NOW SERVES VARIOUS PURPOSES – RESIDENTIAL, OFFICE, ELECTRONICS LABORATORY AND WORKSHOP.

PAST: THE FACTORY WAS BUILT IN 1920 AND IS CONSTRUCTED ENTIRELY OF CONCRETE.

Workshop
Office and electronics lab module
Living room area
Kitchen and dining area

HOTEL PALISADE SYDNEY AUSTRALIA
THE SOCIETY INC BY SIBELLA COURT 2016

Bar taps pay homage to tradesmen
Bar counter

The new design of Hotel Palisade reveals the journey of this building through time. The building's original character is manifested in the ground floor bar, which pays homage to the early days of the local harbor with its hustle and bustle. This was a thriving place where hand-crafted goods were traded, goods that inspired the design of this most recent development. Every item is bespoke and handcrafted by locally based master craftsmen and tradesmen. The fixtures and finishes are also a nod to this industrial past, incorporating simple materials such as zinc, steel, leather, canvas, copper and timber. Listening closely, the visitor might even hear the jeers of the larrikins and the wharfies coming to drink after a day waiting for ships to dock.

Beneath the layers of modern design, there is a ruggedness to this space that chimes perfectly with the historical character of the environment and the eclectic community bound by camaraderie that lived here. The color palette was inspired by both the spectacular views of the waters and the many shades of green found in the original tiles lining the interior walls.

NOW: THE SOCIETY INC BY SIBELLA COURT TRANSFORMED THIS BUILDING INTO AN ACCOMMODATION FOR HOTEL PALISADE, AS WELL AS CREATING BOTH DOWNSTAIRS AND ROOFTOP BARS. SPREAD ACROSS 100 SQUARE METERS, THE MAIN MATERIALS USED INCLUDE ZINC, COPPER, STEEL AND TIMBER.

PAST: HOTEL PALISADE IS A BRICK BUILDING CONSTRUCTED IN 1915 BY HENRY DEANE WALSH WITH THE GROUND FLOOR PUBLIC BAR WRAPPING AROUND ITS FRONT FAÇADE WITH ITS ORIGINAL GLAZED TILES.

Bar seating
Recycled tools used for table numbers
Menu and cutlery
Bar counter

79

OTTO'S NR. 4
HAMBURG
GERMANY
BFGF DESIGN
STUDIOS
2016

Entrance area with view on timber house
Otto's façade

Otto's Burger, a restaurant in Hamburg's popular Schanze quarter, was designed to echo the feel of this particularly trendy area of the city. The former city gate was first enclosed on both sides with glass, and the area transformed into the home of a catering business.

BFGF filled this undefined space between exterior and interior with an iconographic wooden structure that can be used as a dining area. In its materiality, the design of the interior – a novel interpretation of New Vintage Style – generates multiple connections between the various different areas of the restaurant. Original elements are accentuated through the use of vibrant colors, and the selection of materials generates stark divisions between newly installed and original fixtures, while still contributing to a coherent overall design. The interior spaces are bright, with high ceilings. The old, the jaded and the derelict meet the renovated and the gentrified in this restaurant – a sumptuous space generating a variety of different ambiences while truly reflecting the character of the Schanze quarter.

NOW: BFGF DESIGN STUDIOS CONVERTED THIS BUILDING ON SCHANZENSTRASSE FOR OTTO'S BURGER AS A HIGHLY INDIVIDUAL AND UNUSUAL RESTAURANT. THE ORIGINAL BUILDING WAS TRANSFORMED BY USING WOOD, WOOD-BASED MATERIALS, CERAMIC AND STEEL.

PAST: THE ORIGINAL RESIDENTIAL AND OFFICE BUILDING WAS BUILT BY JOHANN GOTTFRIED RAMBATZ AND WILHELM JOLASSE IN 1895 FOR JOHANN MICHAEL FETT & CO. INDUSTRIAL RED BRICK AND GRANITE WERE THE PRIMARY MATERIALS USED.

Bar counter with raw wall structure in background
Dining area in front of bar
Tables and neon sign
Ground floor plan
Interior design and furniture

83

HUESO GUADALA-JARA MEXICO

CADENA + ASOCIADOS

CONCEPT DESIGN 2014

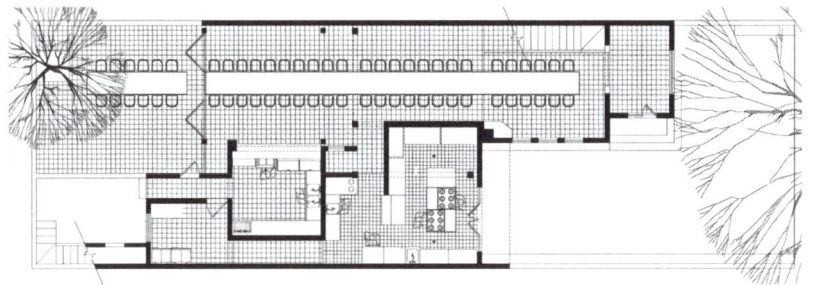

Restaurant table in front of bone wall
Entrance to restaurant
Floor plan

Luis Barragan's Foundation and Diaz Morales' House Studio in the beautiful Lafayette Design District in Guadalajara, Mexico served as the perfect backdrop for a 22-square-meters, 1940s building that was to become Alfonso Cadena's new concept restaurant Hueso, the Spanish word for bone.

The designers began by creating a double skin on the building's exterior. A clean, artisanal, handmade ceramic tile covering protects the inner layer, which is more organic and textured. Inspired by Darwinian ideas, the interior surfaces feature over 10,000 animal bones and plant elements mounted on wooden layers, intermingled with various objects and cooking tools, and covering every vertical square centimeter. Several urban visual artists were involved in this unusually creative intervention.

NOW: CADENA + ASOCIADOS CONCEPT DESIGN RE-ESTABLISHED THIS BUILDING FOR ALFONSO CADENA AS A CONCEPT RESTAURANT. SPREAD ACROSS 22 SQUARE METERS, THE ORIGINAL ART STUDIO IS NOW MAINLY USED FOR MEETING, EATING AND DRINKING.

PAST: THE ORIGINAL RESIDENTIAL BUILDING WAS ERECTED IN THE 1940S, USED AS AN ART STUDIO BY THE LUIS BARRAGAN'S FOUNDATION. THE MAIN CONSTRUCTION MATERIALS USED WERE CONCRETE AND TILES.

Bone wall
Table in front of bone wall
Animal skull on partly renewed wall
Restaurant table beneath gallery

86

SABOC
BARCELONA
SPAIN
VENTURA
ESTUDIO
ADAM
BRESNICK
ARCHITECTS
2013

Perspective
Building exterior
Seating area

The restaurant, transformed by Juan Carlos Fernandez, Reyes Castellano and Adam Bresnick, along with Antonio Romeo and Miguel Peña, is located on a prominent corner facing the recently restored Born Cultural Center, the old Mercat del Born. The food is based on four types of cooking and is the protagonist, while the architectural intervention is a discreet and fitting backdrop.

The space has been stripped and the original brick and ashlar stone exposed. The former is painted a warm gray to create a more uniform container. The floor uses an encaustic tile typical of the nineteenth century, with a play of gray hexagons that recall the paving of the Passeig de Gracia, giving character to the space. The fixed elements are birch plywood, stained a light white to soften the esthetic. Indirect lighting and warm gray upholstery create a cozy ambience. The furniture is of Nordic influence, with soft lines and noble materials that stand out. An ochre fabric adds contrast to the interior.

NOW: VENTURA ESTUDIO AND ADAM BRESNICK ARCHITECTS REFURBISHED THIS BUILDING FOR THE SABOC RESTAURANT, CREATING A MODERN AND EXTRAORDINARY ATMOSPHERE. 250 SQUARE METERS WERE TRANSFORMED BY USING ENCAUSTIC TILE, BIRCH PLYWOOD AND EXPOSED PAINTED BRICK.

PAST: THE ORIGINAL RESIDENTIAL BUILDING AND STORE WAS ERECTED IN THE LATE NINETEENTH CENTURY, AND WAS CHARACTERIZED BY THE USE OF GRANITE AND BRICK.

New bar
View of old market
Restaurant area downstairs
Group tables

PATISSERIE III
MADRID
SPAIN

IDEO
ARQUI-
TECTURA
2015

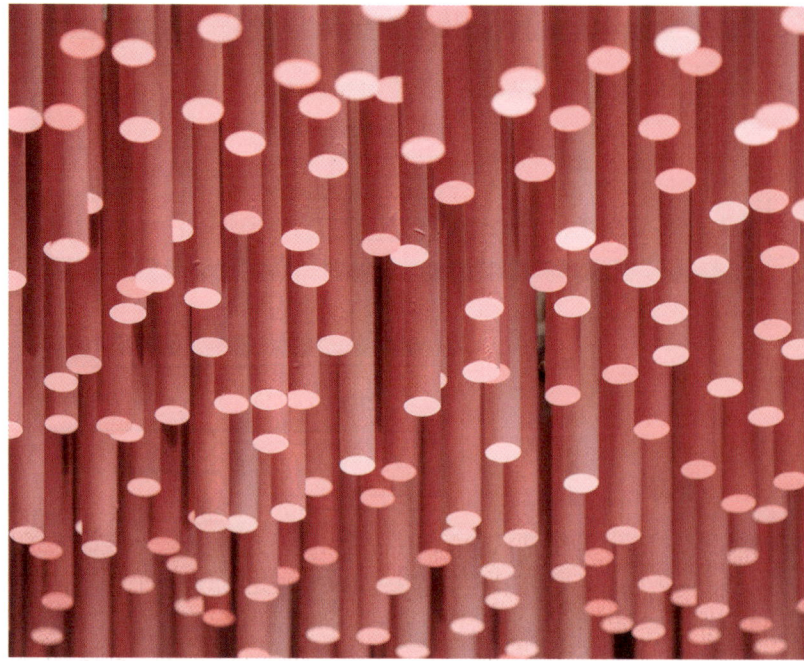

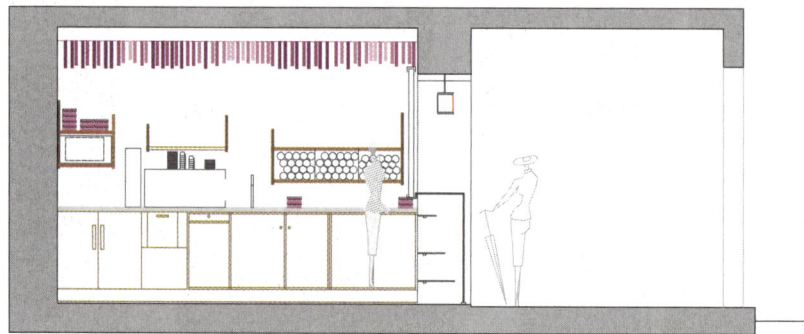

Detail of wooden magenta sticks
Section
Counter at entrance

The architect was commissioned to design the third branch of Pan y Pasteles bakery in Madrid. The client was keen for each of the bakeries to have a unique esthetic, while always incorporating the brand color magenta and achieving a contemporary look. The historic building is located in the old center of Alcala de Henares. After demolishing the internal walls and cleaning up the façade, the architects decided to keep new features to a minimum – the existing brick walls were in good condition and exuded a great deal of character suitable for a modern bakery.

Their task was to design an element with an equally strong character that could complement the original features. The result was a magnificent artistic installation, comprising more than 12,000 wooden magenta sticks that have been hung from the ceiling. The architect, Virginia del Barco, also designed the lighting, some of the furniture – including the chairs, stools, shelves and bar top – and the light boxes in the façades. Details in the cladding lend the space a refined elegance.

NOW: SPREAD ACROSS 55 SQUARE METERS, IDEO ARQUITECTURA GAVE THE VAULTED ROOMS FOR PAN Y PASTELES A MODERN LOOK USING WOODEN MAGENTA STICKS.

PAST: THIS 150-YEAR-OLD STRUCTURE ON CALLE MAYOR, 3 ALCALÁ DE HENARES IN MADRID COMPRISES MAINLY WOOD AND BRICKS.

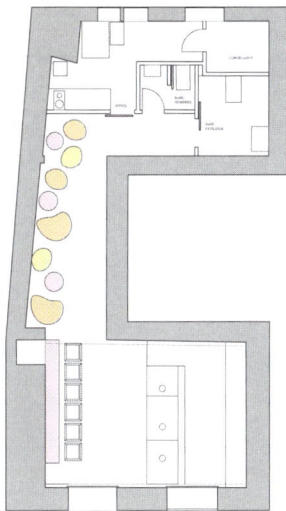

Shop window
Corridor with seating
Counter
Floor plan
Seating in front of historical brickwork

95

ANTIVILLA KRAMPNITZ GERMANY

BRANDLHU-
BER+ EMDE,
BURLON
2014

Kitchen and dining area
Building exterior with concrete roof

Renovated by Arno Brandlhuber and used as a multipurpose residence, the Antivilla is located next to a lake near Potsdam. The local branch of the East German factory, Ernst Lück Wittstock, has been transformed into a living and atelier building along with a display area for art. A central element of the design is the renovation of the roof, which had to be replaced by a concrete surface and features a water spout that projects dramatically into the air.

Openings on the gable end of the building have been added and generate views of the natural surroundings from the interior. A concrete core has also been added, housing the bathrooms and kitchen, as well as a sauna and fireplace. In winter, the 200-square-meter open space can be subdivided by a curtain, reducing the surface to approximately 75 square meters. Ecological and social concerns were at the heart of this unconventional renovation project. The old East German trappings have been preserved. All in all, Antivilla was created as a hedonistic project that is characterized above all by the versatility of its functions and its alternative approach to current standards of living.

NOW: BRANDLHUBER+ EMDE, BURLON TRANSFORMED THIS OLD EAST GERMAN BUILD-ING INTO A RESIDENTIAL AND ATELIER SPACE TO BE USED BY ARNO BRANDLHUBER. WITH A 1,466-SQUARE-METER PLOT AND A 445-SQUARE-METER FLOOR AREA, THE LOFT-LIKE HOUSE OFFERS A RANGE OF POSSIBLE FUNCTIONS.

PAST: THIS ORIGINAL INDUSTRIAL BUILDING BELONGING TO THE FIRM ERNST LÜCK WITTSTOCK WAS BUILT IN THE EARLY 1980S. IT WAS CHARACTERIZED THEN, AS IT IS NOW, BY ITS RAW CONCRETE-LIKE EXTERIOR.

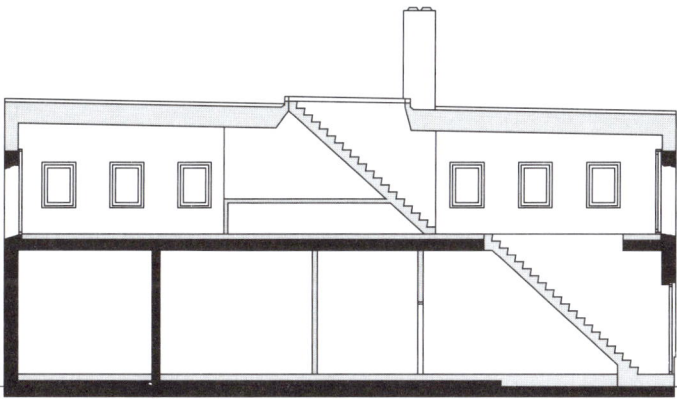

Entrance to top level
Lake view from inside
Living area
Section
Fireplace

TROU NORMAND SAN FRANCISCO CA, USA

BOOR BRIDGES ARCHITECTURE 2014

Exterior patio with custom steel and glass trellis
View of the bar as one enters

The name Trou Normand means "Normandy Gap" and refers to the traditional pause in a meal in Normandy when one takes a moment to have a glass of Calvados before continuing to eat. Trou Normand is a bar, butchery and a restaurant all in one.

A modern riff on the beauty of Art Deco, the design employs distilled details alongside bold commentary. The architects kept the brick and concrete bones of the building, and layered on wood and leather design elements to set the tone for the comfortable, inviting nature of the establishment. They began the design process with a thorough study and conceptual analysis of period art, entertainment and interpretations, which led them to a robust, integral, sensory palette of materials. The space is on the ground floor of an iconic Art Deco high-rise designed by Timothy Pflueger, which underwent extensive interior remodeling. Trou Normand's space includes a new exterior patio with a steel and glass trellis.

NOW: TROU NORMAND IS A BAR AND RESTAURANT AT 140 NEW MONTGOMERY STREET, SAN FRANSISCO. BOOR BRIDGES ARCHITECTURE DESIGNED THE 232-SQUARE-METER SPACE USING RECLAIMED MARBLE, WOOD, STEEL, PLASTER, LEATHER AND CONCRETE TILES.

PAST: THE FORMER OFFICE BUILDING OF THE PACIFIC TELEGRAPH COMPANY WAS BUILT BY TIMOTHY PFLUEGER IN 1925, USING CONCRETE, STONE AND STEEL.

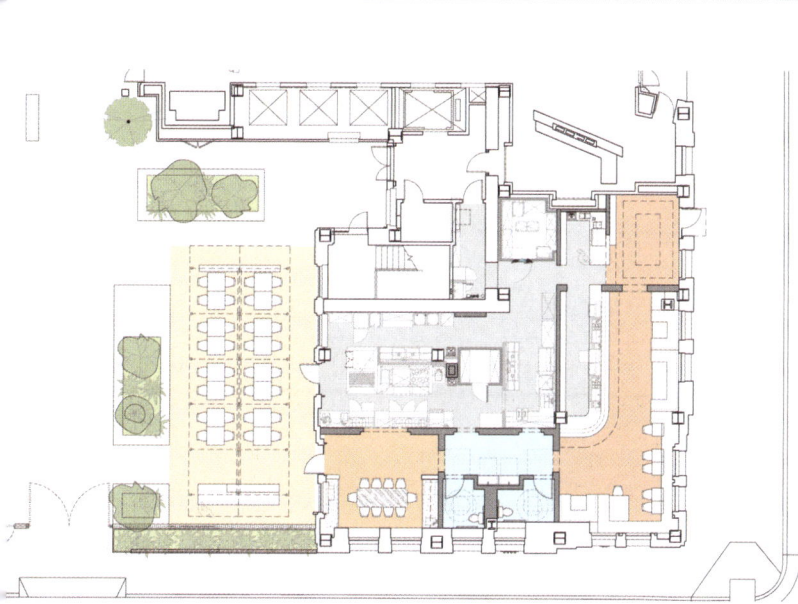

Looking back towards the bar and entry
Marble reclaimed from lobbies on top of the bar and custom purse hooks made of leather
Butcher's table by day, chef's table by night
Floor plan
Bathroom doors reclaimed from stairwells

STAR BURGER KIEV UKRAINE SERGEY MAKHNO ARCHITECTS 2016

The restaurant is designed to appeal to a wide audience
Restaurant interior

Combining sophisticated design and a cozy atmosphere was the key aim of the architects responsible for the Star Burger project. In response to their client's wish, they based their visual strategy on the brand's colors of black and green. One of the central challenges was the creation of an environment that was both comfortable and functional.

The resulting design is spread over two floors and comprises a series of open and versatile spaces. The ground floor zones are intended for socializing, while the upper floor invites relaxation and has been dubbed "the family one" because of its soft furniture and warm atmosphere. The two floors are connected via a giant wooden portal, which also brings additional light into the interior. Fifty light fittings illuminate the restaurant and multiple elements are juxtaposed in a harmonious composition. Clay chandeliers of varying sizes and shapes are just one example of this. Inspired by the esthetic qualities of bees and by soft lines, they generate an authentic and natural atmosphere. A unique wall light complements these chandeliers, enhancing the loft-like feel of the space.

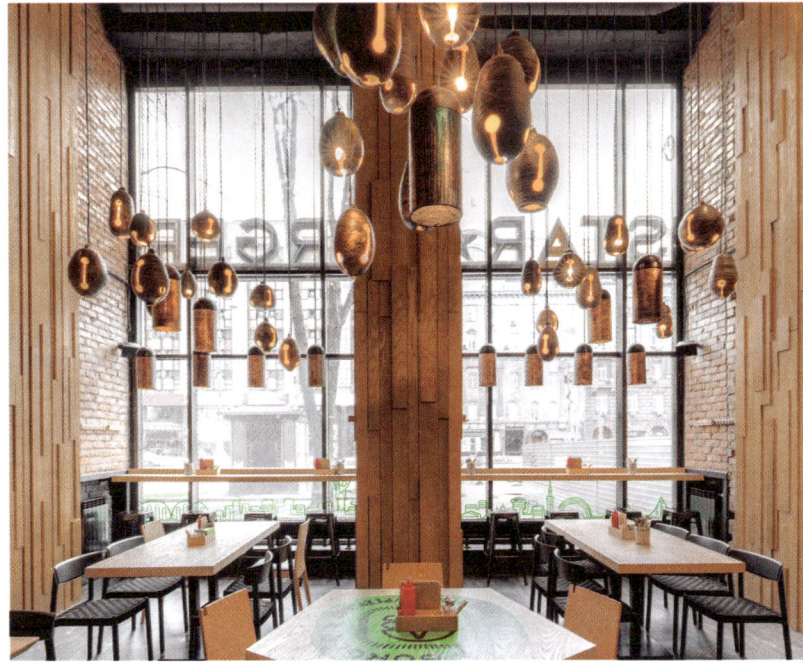

NOW: SERGEY MAKHNO ARCHITECTS RENEWED THIS BUILDING FOR STAR BURGER AS A HIP NEW RESTAURANT WITH A COZY ATMOSPHERE. SPREAD ACROSS 315 SQUARE METERS, THE HISTORICAL BUILDING WAS CONVERTED BY USING A UNIQUE LIGHT AND DESIGN CONCEPT.

PAST: THE ORIGINAL BANK BUILDING WAS ERECTED BY VOLODYMYR ZABOLOTNYI AND NATALIIA CHMUTINA FOR THE CENTRAL UNION OF CONSUMER SOCIETIES OF UKRAINE FROM 1954 TO 1957. BRICKS WERE THE MAIN MATERIAL USED IN THE CONSTRUCTION PROCESS.

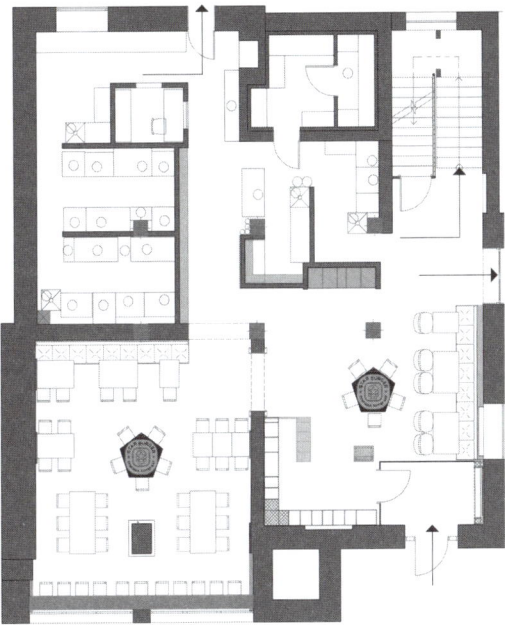

Bar tables with suspension luminaires
Lighting design draws attention of visitors
Brick walls with detailed decoration
First floor plan
Classic American bar atmosphere

107

PERRY STREET LOFT NEW YORK CITY NY, USA TANG KAWASAKI STUDIO 2006

Vaulted brick ceilings
Loft view

The architects were commissioned to restore and reconfigure an apartment in Greenwich Village. New partitions have been added that merge with the white interior canvas, while close attention has also been paid to the finishing and compositional framing of the existing floor and ceiling surfaces. The former industrial building's brick ceilings have been balanced by bleaching and desaturating existing white oak floors.

Below, teak casement windows, radiators and storage units are enclosed by perforated lacquer millwork. White gypsum volumes concealed various programs, ranging from a laundry station to a built-in study. The living areas shift and overlap between two monumentally proportioned walls. A tall kitchen island wall shields expansive stainless steel counters from the main living areas, which are characterized by the play of natural light, complemented by the warm washed walls and incandescent globes. Bedrooms and their accessory functions have been concealed behind massive plaster walls with reductive details set in subtle contrast with the omnipresent brick ceilings. An original wood burning fireplace has been restored and appropriated into the new master bedroom.

NOW: THE PERRY STREET LOFT WAS RESTORED AND RECONFIGURED FOR A YOUNG FAMILY OF FOUR. WITH A FLOOR AREA OF 148 SQUARE METERS, THE BUILDING FOR CO-OPERATIVE HOUSING WAS TRANSFORMED WITH BRICK, PLASTER AND WHITE OAK.

PAST: THE ORIGINAL WAREHOUSE WAS BUILT IN 1905 USING BRICK MASONRY UNITS.

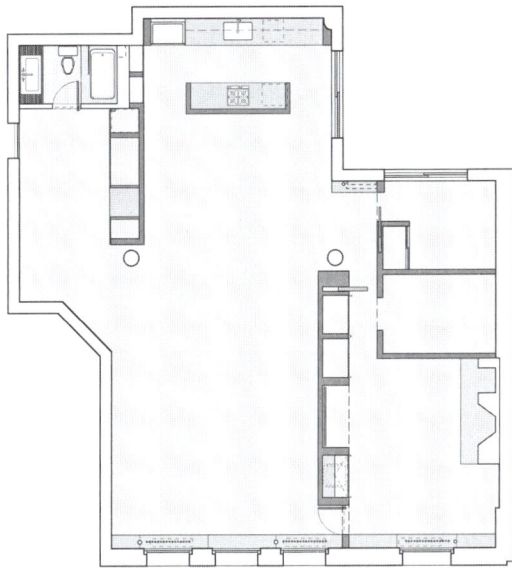

Fireplace
Bedroom alcove
View from kitchen
Floor plan
Foyer and bathroom

CHESA GABRIEL SAMEDAN SWITZER-LAND CORINNA MENN 2013

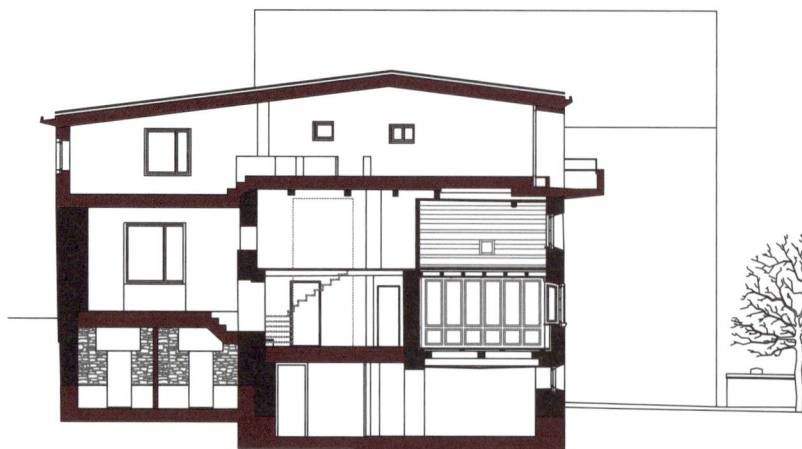

Section
Kitchen and dining room
Exterior view

Chesa Gabriel lies above and to the north-west of Samedan's church square and is part of a historical body of urban development. The physical structure tells the story of a series of renovations and expansions that have defined the building's development over centuries; a manifestation of architectural continuity. Originally a farm dwelling complete with stable, it has now been transformed into a duplex. The house was dismantled to reveal the original wooden floor and beams, while vertical elements like stairs, bathrooms, and the utility shaft have been carefully added.

The original structure forms the basis of the design for the ground and first floors, while the upper story, subject to a twentieth century expansion that eradicated the historical structure, has been reinterpreted as an open-plan space. Each of the interventions contributes to an overall impression of perfect unity between the existing and new elements. The house retains an aura of the ancient and yet emerges as a wholly contemporary dwelling space.

NOW: AFTER COUNTLESS RENOVATIONS AND CONVERSIONS, THIS HISTORICAL BUILDING IS NOW USED AS A DUPLEX. WITH THIS TRANSFORMATION BY CORINNA MENN, THE STRUCTURE ACQUIRES A CONTEMPORARY CHARACTER.

PAST: THIS OLD RURAL HOUSE WAS ORIGINALLY BUILT IN THE SIXTEENTH CENTURY. KEY CHARACTERISTICS ARE THE LONG NARROW PLOT, THE ORIGINAL BARN AND THE EXTENSIVE USE OF WOOD.

Basement
Living area
Bedroom
Balcony

ROUGH LUXE HOTEL LONDON ENGLAND RABIH HAGE 2008

Guest room with gilded headboard and Massimo Listri photo above
Bathtub and uncovered hand-painted wallpaper

The Rough Luxe Hotel is a blend of urban archaeology elements, including partially sanded surfaces, bare floorboards, chipped paint and rough edges mixed with contemporary wallpaper and art, plus top quality furnishings. The building was also previously operated as a hotel by an Italian family. As a listed building from the 1850s, there were limits to the scope of the redevelopment. Early on in the refurbishment, layers of wallpaper were peeled away to reveal decoration from centuries ago. Rabih Hage's instinct was to preserve this intriguing "archaeology" of interior design.

In each room the "deconstructed" walls contrast with contemporary or trompe l'oeil wallpapers created from photographs of interiors by Massimo Listri, generating an illusion of space and opulence. The "luxe" element of the hotel can be seen and felt in the top quality beds as well as the fine linen and characteristic furniture. The hotel is the ultimate statement in urban archaeology, where old and new can collide and blend.

NOW: RABIH HAGE RE-ESTABLISHED THE BUILDING AS A HOTEL, WITH A FLOOR AREA OF 205 SQUARE METERS. THE ARCHITECTS SANDED DOWN AND CAREFULLY REMOVED FIVE TO SIX LAYERS OF PLASTER AND WALLPAPER TO REVEAL THE MANY LAYERS.

PAST: THE ORIGINAL TERRACED HOUSE WAS BUILT IN THE 1850S. BRICK, TIMBER AND PLASTER WERE THE PRIMARY MATERIALS USED TO BUILD IT.

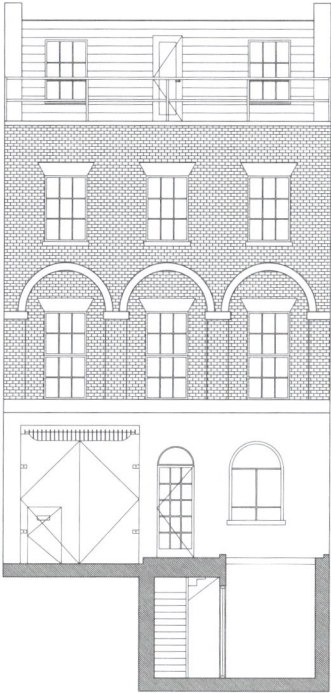

Former guest room converted into shower room
Daybed and wardrobe
Daybed
Elevation
Lobby and reception room

119

A LINE BETWEEN TIME

BEIJING CHINA

CUN-DESIGN
2016

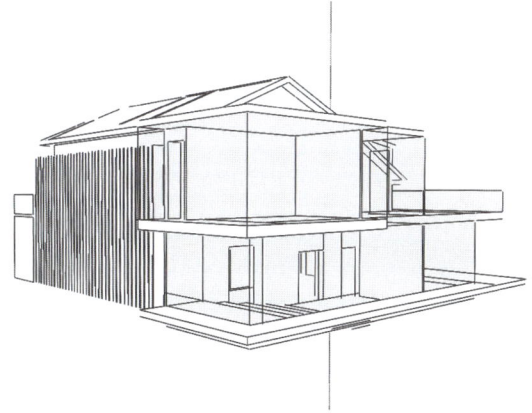

Corridor consisting of opaque glass plate
Perspective
External façade

This building is located on the bank of Wen-Yu River in East Beijing. During the renovation, Cun-Design preserved the original structure and formed a contrasting boundary between old and new within the project. The design integrates outdoor with indoor areas, allowing the space to return to its original nature.

To maximize the use of space, the interior heat preservation elements have been removed and the original red brick structure exposed. All doors, removable walls and windowsills were removed and all of the rooms connected. Mirrors were integrated to hide the pillars and expand the visual dimension through reflection. The bathroom retained its original rough surface, while the sink was pushed into the wall and a mirror inserted to generate a sense of spaciousness. The original stairs were removed and a glass box corridor built in their place. Contrasts between old and new are at the heart of the project and lend it a unique beauty.

NOW: CUN-DESIGN RENOVATED THIS BUILDING FOR BLUE MOON CULTURE AS AN OFFICE. SPREAD ACROSS 500 SQUARE METERS, THE ORIGINAL RESIDENTIAL BUILDING IS NOW MAINLY USED FOR ORGANIZING FILMS.

PAST: THE FORMER SINGLE-FAMILY VILLA WAS BUILT AT THE END OF THE 1990S. MAINLY RED BRICKS AND CONCRETE WERE USED FOR THE CONSTRUCTION.

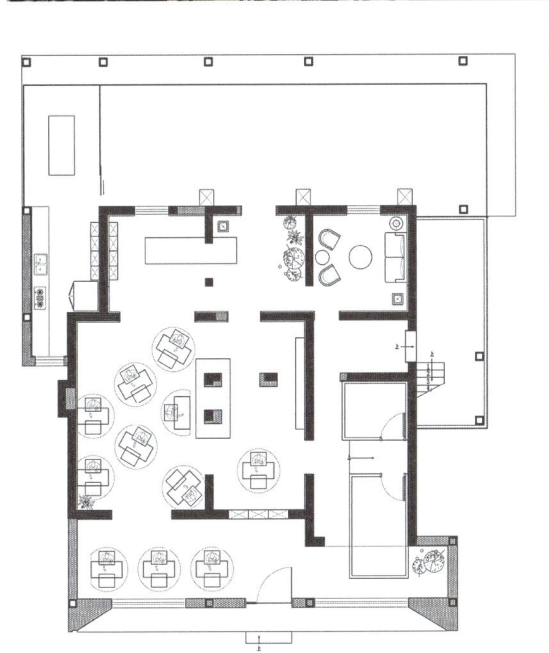

Brick wall and wooden structure
Exposed brickwork construction
Wall consisting of clapperboards
Ground floor plan
Rough walls used as mirror frames in the bathroom

STUDIO FUKSAS ROME ITALY

FUKSAS

2017

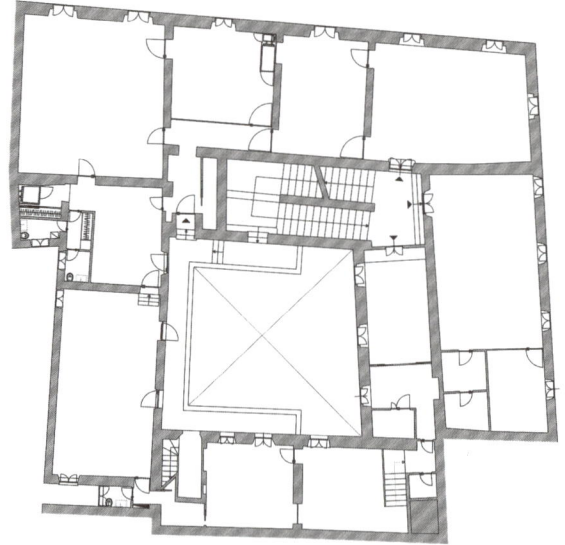

First floor plan
Glimpse of exhibition space and archive room
Interior of historical palace housing Studio Fuksas

Fuksas' atelier in Rome is situated in a Renaissance building on Piazza del Monte di Pietà, near Campo dei Fiori. The atelier has four floors and hosts offices, design rooms, a model-making room and meeting rooms. A lift with an iron platform, crystal walls and natural steel fixtures connects the first floor with the aquarium room, where meetings take place.

In some parts of the atelier, the lime plaster walls have been renovated in order to amplify the layers of plaster and paint added over time. Hanging on the walls are several models shielded in showcases as well as paintings and sketches by Massimiliano Fuksas. Among the atelier's furniture are various pieces by Fuksas, such as the table "Tommaso" for Zeus, the office chair "Bea" for Luxy, the corporate table "Mumbai" for Haworth Castelli, and the table "Biennale Collection" for Saporiti. Several design classics are also featured, including the "Panton Chair" by Verner Panton, the "Lounge Chair" by Charles Eames, the chair "Ant" by Arne Jacobsen, and the table series "B637" by Hein, Mathsson and Jacobsen.

NOW: FUKSAS RENOVATED THE BUILDING NEAR CAMPO DEI FIORI BUT KEPT THE SPIRIT OF THE CENTURIES ALIVE. THE ATELIER HAS AN AREA OF 1,100 SQUARE METERS, SPREAD OVER FOUR FLOORS. USED AS A LABORATORY, THE RENOVATION IS STILL IN PROGRESS.

PAST: THE PRESENT CONFIGURATION OF THE RENAISSANCE BUILDING DATES BACK TO THE SECOND HALF OF THE NINETEENTH CENTURY.

Meeting room with models kept in display cases
Restored interior walls in work space
Private office of Massimiliano Fuksas
Furniture designed by Doriana and Massimiliano Fuksas
Model in work space with exposed ceilings

VEGAN HOUSE
HO CHI MINH
VIETNAM
BLOCK
ARCHITECTS
2014

Section
Frontal view from outside
Dining room with table

Starting from the premise that new things can be created by rearranging the old, the architects succeeded in creating a space where past and present, old and new, support and enhance each other.

The old windows become a central feature, contributing to the distinctive appearance of the dwelling and ensuring good ventilation of the interior. They have been rearranged into a new and colorful façade that wraps the original façade from the ground all the way up to the rooftop. Inside the house, these windows function as partitions bringing light into the space, separating and decorating individual interior areas. A new steel staircase, built next to the atrium, leads to the second floor, which was previously an unused roof area. A bedroom made of old steel sheeting was also added just beneath the roof. The original material of the walls and floors has been largely preserved, including unrefined cement surfaces, jalousie windows and bamboo wattle on the ceiling, generating a place that is both ancient and modern and reviving 1960s and 1970s traditions of Vietnamese architecture.

NOW: BLOCK ARCHITECTS RENOVATED THE BUILDING FOR TAM NGUYEN AS A CULTURAL PLACE. SPREAD ACROSS 60 SQUARE METERS, THE ORIGINAL OLD TERRACE HOUSE IS NOW MAINLY USED AS A MEETING POINT AS WELL AS A SPACE FOR COOKING AND EATING VEGAN VIETNAMESE FOOD.

PAST: THE ORIGINAL OLD TERRACE HOUSE WAS BUILT IN 1965. HOA BON HUA USED THE BUILDING FOR RESIDENTIAL PURPOSES. THE FORMER BUILDING WAS CONSTRUCTED MAINLY OF CONCRETE AND BRICK.

Corridor with washbasin made of old sewing machine
Roof windows provide trees with natural light
Seating area
Old staircase

P BLOK
PRODUCTION
STUDIO
ISTANBUL
TURKEY
IGLO
ARCHITECTS
2010

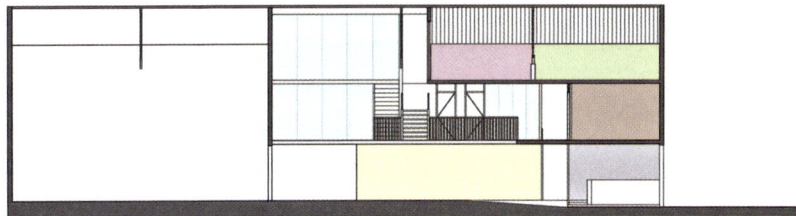

Hallway with 8-meter high ceiling
Section
Entrance

This warehouse was transformed into a photography and production studio, which also contains office and café functions. The project was designed around contrasting aspects such as permeability and isolation between spaces, light and dark, and black and white. Careful planning ensures that the functional spaces – offices, post-production, and studio areas – are in spatial harmony with the supportive spaces such as the café, make-up room, storage room and bathroom facilities. Gray and transparent glass surfaces and warm wood in the furnishings and upper story floorings complement the black-and-white background.

The old façade was transformed by a simple layer of paint. A new entrance door was added in the reception area and two additional stories were installed at the side. At the rear, two studios take full advantage of the high ceilings. The office next door was being moved, so the structural steel elements there were removed and reused in this project, giving this renovation an economical and sustainably character.

NOW: IGLO ARCHITECTS RE-ESTABLISHED THE BUILDING FOR P BLOK/UTOPIA FOTOGRAF PRODUKSIYON AS OFFICE. SPREAD ACROSS 450 SQUARE METERS, THE ORIGINAL WAREHOUSE IS NOW USED FOR CREATING VISUAL SOLUTIONS. STEEL, GLASS, GYPSUM PANELS, EPOXY, AND WOOD WERE THE MAIN MATERIALS USED DURING CONSTRUCTION.

PAST: THE ORIGINAL WAREHOUSE WAS BUILT WITH A STEEL SKELETON AND SANDWICH PANELS.

Studio
Stairs
Kitchen
Ground floor plan
First mezzanine floor plan
Mezzanine floors

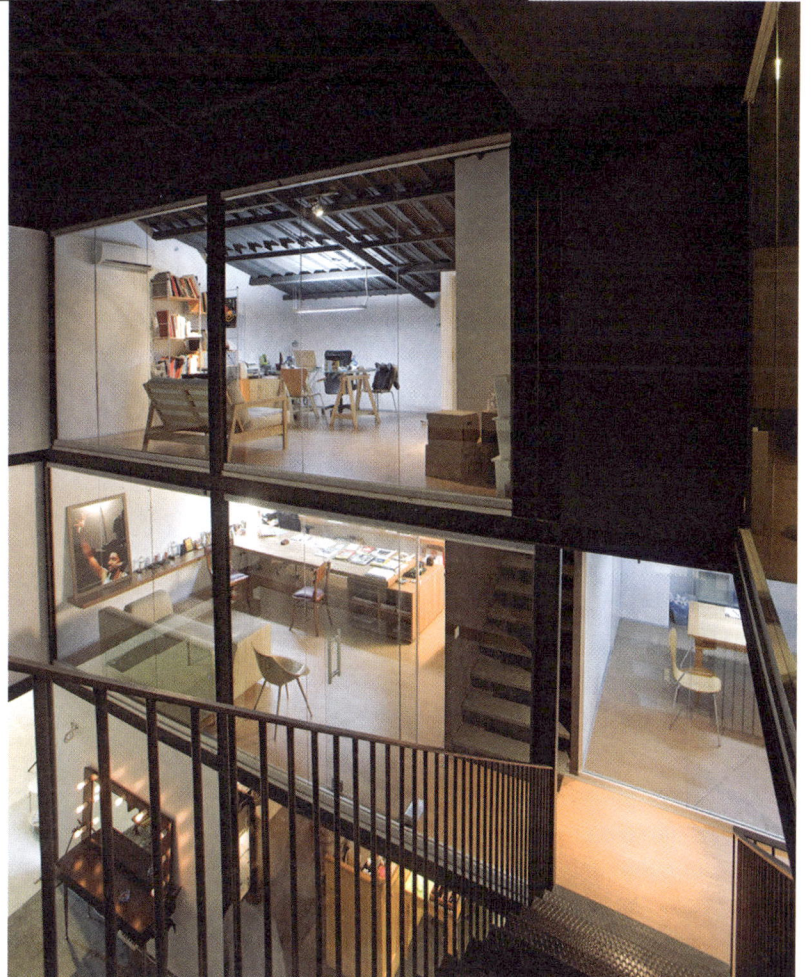

TOKYO LOFT
TOKYO
JAPAN
G ARCHITECTS
STUDIO
SUMA-SAGA-
FUDOSAN
2014

View of kitchen
Bathroom
Loft area

This unique apartment is located in the very heart of Tokyo, in an attic featuring long, sloping ceilings and a raw interior. The slanted ceilings were converted into a skylight allowing sunlight to flood the space and generating a spectacular and unobstructed view of the city. In order to achieve harmony between the industrial attic interior and a welcoming hotel-like atmosphere, soft painting techniques inspired by traditional Japanese paper ("Washi") were used on the surface of the raw concrete walls and ceilings. This hotel apartment was conceived as a test model for future projects, offering a welcome alternative to central Tokyo's existing hotel industry.

During the 1980s, Japan's economic bubble created a host of "pencil buildings." These were tall, slender structures built to utilize small plots of land in Tokyo for maximum profitability. This project is rejuvenating these existing structures, breathing new life into old buildings.

NOW: RYOHEI TANAKA FROM G ARCHITECTS STUDIO AND TERUYA KIDO FROM SUMA-SAGA-FUDOSAN RE-ESTABLISHED THE BUILDING AS A LOFT BY USING RESIN SHEETS AND CONCRETE. SPREAD ACROSS ALMOST 60 SQUARE METERS, IT IS NOW MAINLY USED FOR ACCOMMODATION PURPOSES.

PAST: CONSTRUCTED MAINLY OF CONCRETE, THIS HOUSING COMPLEX WAS BUILT IN 1977.

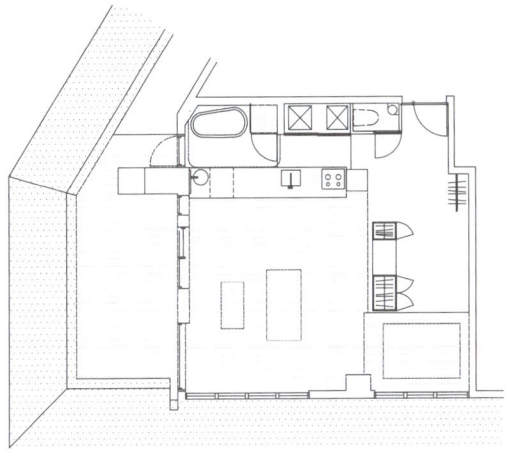

Toilet and sink
Sloped ceiling
View from kitchen
Floor plan
Concrete pillar and kitchen

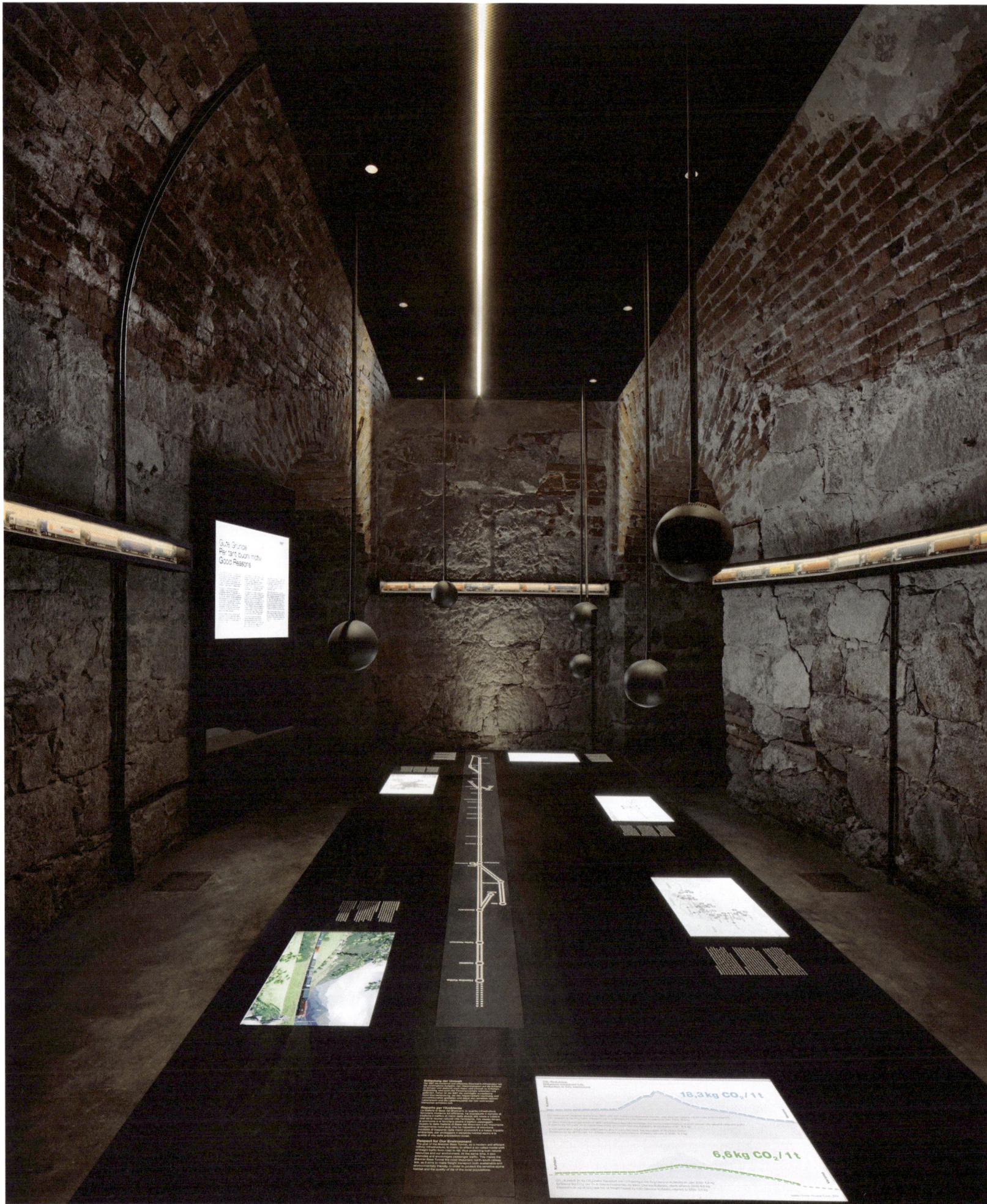

Gute Gründe
Per tanti buoni motivi
Good Reasons

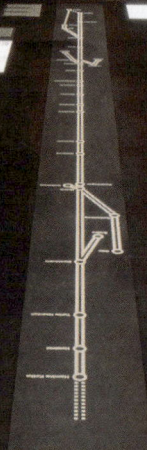

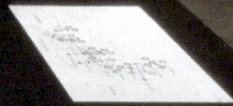

Entlastung der Umwelt

Rispetto per l'Ambiente

Respect for Our Environment

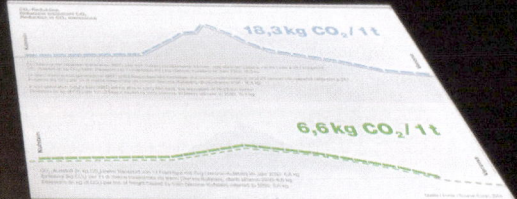

18,3 kg CO₂ / 1 t

6,6 kg CO₂ / 1 t

FRANZENS-FESTE FOR-TIFICATION BOLZANO ITALY

MARKUS SCHERER ARCHITEKT 2016

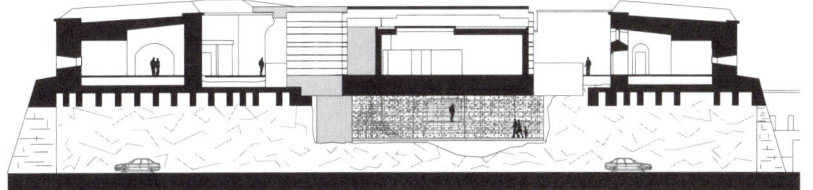

Exhibition
Section showing Brenner state street below fortification
Multi-purpose hall with courtyard

This project involved the renovation and extension of the last of three independent sections of the fort – structure C and information point BBT.

The preservation of certain elements, combined with minimal interventions, are intended to give the building a more functional character. The materials were selected to establish a dialogue with the existing structure. The palette of materials was kept minimal and simple, allowing the new elements to blend harmoniously with the historical context. The new structure was realized as a type of covering above the tunnel entrance. Through this intervention it became possible to make the whole ruin accessible. The new hall was integrated as a room within a room, inside the reconstructed building shell. Previously lost structures have been restored, while the preserved volumes were both restored and enhanced. The new main entrance and a small open foyer area can be found at street level in a covered zone within the new structure. Based on HG Merz's exhibition concept, the architect was also responsible for developing the exhibition, while curator Sebastian Marseiler provided the exhibits.

NOW: THE AUTONOME PROVINCE OF BOLZANO AND BBT SE BRENNERBASISTUNNEL COMMISSIONED MARKUS SCHERER ARCHITEKT TO RECONSTRUCT THE REMAINS AS A MUSEUM, USING MAINLY CONCRETE WITH GRANITE AS AGGREGATE AND GALVANIZED PATINATED STEEL.

PAST: THE FORTIFICATION WAS BUILT USING PRIMARILY GRANITE AND BRICKS BY FRANZ VON SCHOLL AND KARL VON MARTONY FROM 1833 TO 1838 FOR THE AUSTRO-HUNGARIAN EMPIRE UNDER EMPEROR FRANZ I.

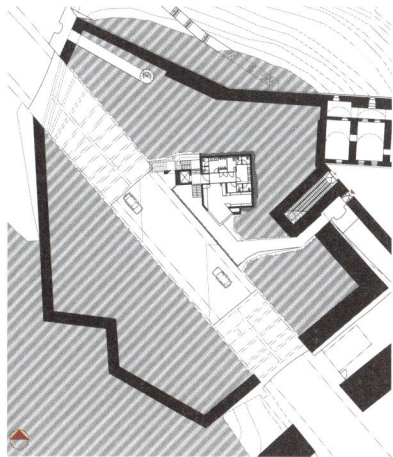

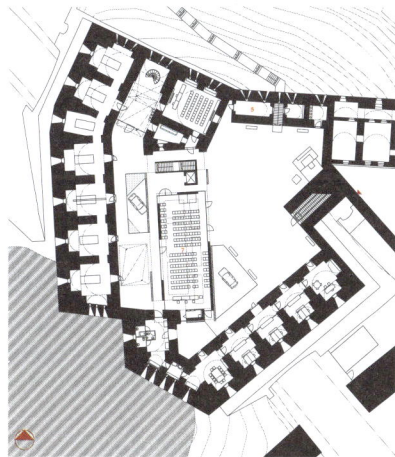

Entrance to exhibition
State street below fortification.
Façade of multi-purpose hall
Floor plan of street and entry level
Floor plan of fortification level
Hall spanning over street

NANDO'S CORK IRELAND STAC ARCHITECTURE 2015

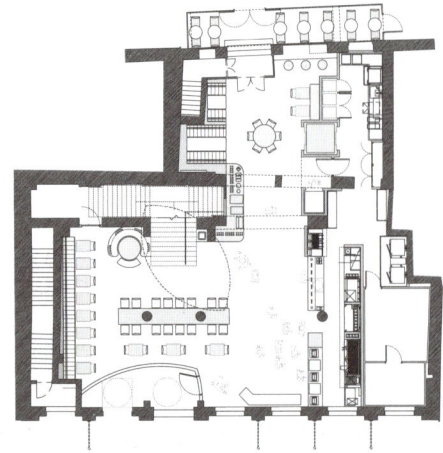

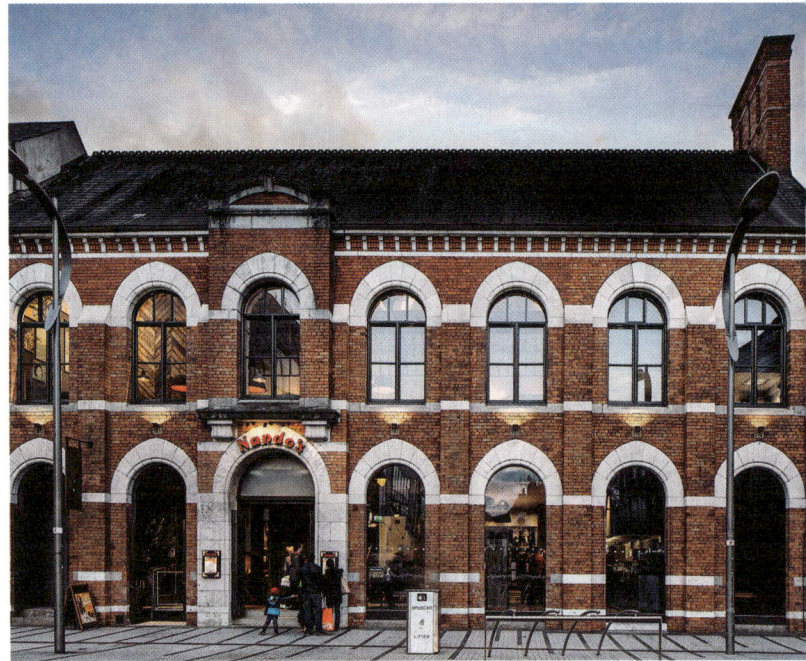

Ground floor plan
View of façade from Academy Street
Concrete drop pendants in front of brick wall

STAC Architecture combined two existing buildings to form a single restaurant space over two levels – a space that respects its former life as a church, whilst creating a new restaurant that is unmistakably Nando's in its materiality and final form.

They opened up the first floor to create a void that would entice customers up the stairs. The existing ceiling was stripped out to reveal king post trusses. Following the strip out of the existing floor, the architects upcycled the timber floorboards to create a new feature, a wall cladding. They also upcycled the existing white painted gallery timber boards used as new cladding to form a new ceiling on the first floor. All timber cladding stripped out of the existing building was impregnated and repurposed as wall and ceiling cladding. A central connecting stair links the ground and first floor as well as the two adjacent buildings. The original masonry has been exposed on the walls and is complemented by external lighting fixtures and a fully glazed roof.

NOW: STAC ARCHITECTURE RE-ESTABLISHED THIS BUILDING FOR NANDO'S UK. SPREAD ACROSS 550 SQUARE METERS, THIS FORMER CHURCH IS NOW USED AS A RESTAURANT.

PAST: THE ORIGINAL CHURCH WAS BUILT IN 1878. SLATE, TERRACOTTA RIDGE CRESTINGS, RED BRICK WALLS AND CHIMNEY, AND GRAY LIMESTONE WERE USED IN THE CONSTRUCTION.

Exposed, painted brickwork wall
Exposed original king post roof trusses
Ground floor dining with communal dining table
Modern furniture and fumed oak floor

147

BAR BROSÉ
SYDNEY
AUSTRALIA
LUCHETTI
KRELLE
2016

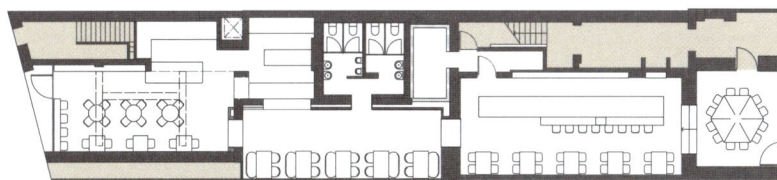

Line of tables
Floor plan
Main bar and kitchen

For Bar Brosé, Luchetti Krelle were commissioned to completely transform the space from what was a very dark and narrow tunnel-like interior into a fresh, open, simplified one. Ambiguity was the guiding concept – the space had to appeal to wine bar drinkers and diners alike.

All of the wall linings were stripped back to reveal the old brickwork and archways previously hidden. The archways now have mirror inserts that are edge lit, creating pools of soft, indirect light and the illusion of space. The backlit glass blocks to the larder are a bold statement, transforming what is usually merely a tool used in architecture into a means of harnessing natural light. Terracotta vents have been stacked and backlit above and below the hot pass with flat steel plate trims. Brass is used throughout as a trim and finishing detail to the simple palette of blue, white and natural timber. The private dining room features a flexible octagonal table that can be broken apart and used in multiple configurations for smaller groups when required.

NOW: LUCHETTI KRELLE TRANSFORMED THIS BUILDING BY USING ARCHITECTURAL GLASS BLOCKS, TERRACOTTA AIR VENTS, TASMANIAN OAK AND BRASS. WITH AN AREA OF 70 SQUARE METERS, IT IS NOW MAINLY USED AS BAR AND RESTAURANT.

PAST: THE ORIGINAL BUILDING WAS ERECTED AT THE END OF THE NINETEENTH CENTURY AND EXTENDED IN THE FIRST HALF OF THE TWENTIETH CENTURY. THE FORMER CONSTRUCTION COMPRISED MAINLY BRICK.

Front bar and kitchen
Private dining
Frontal view of kitchen
Table for four

WHITE HOUSE GULDENTAL GERMANY
PLANUNGS-BÜRO I21
2016

Extension of existing building
Main room

This unusual event location is characterized by a unique interaction between the rural building and the modern architectural form of the annex. The homely atmosphere and raw character of the old barn, used as a stable for horses, were preserved by exposing and restoring the brickwork in a labor-intensive intervention.

Along with a new oak parquet floor and improved acoustics, the space also acquired a charming element in the bar area – a bronze counter, its edges softened by the atmospheric, ambient lighting. Flooded with light, esthetically purist and embracing a simple formal language, the new annex, named White House, contrasts the main building, while appearing to emerge from it and generating a fresh overall impression of the site's architecture. Large windows offer views of the idyllic countryside surrounding the property, while a seamless cement floor and reserved color palette combined with a simple lighting plan and minimal built-in furniture generate a compelling esthetic interaction between old and new.

NOW: PLANUNGSBÜRO I21 UNDER DIRECTION OF INTERIOR ARCHITECT HEIKO GRUBER RENOVATED THE BUILDING FOR THE BUCHHOLZ FAMILY BY USING BRICK MASONRY, PARQUET FLOORING AND CEMENT. SPREAD ACROSS 260 SQUARE METERS, THE FORMER HORSE STABLE IS NOW MAINLY USED AS AN EVENT LOCATION.

PAST: THE ORIGINAL HORSE STABLE WAS BUILT IN 1900, USING MAINLY BRICK AND WOOD.

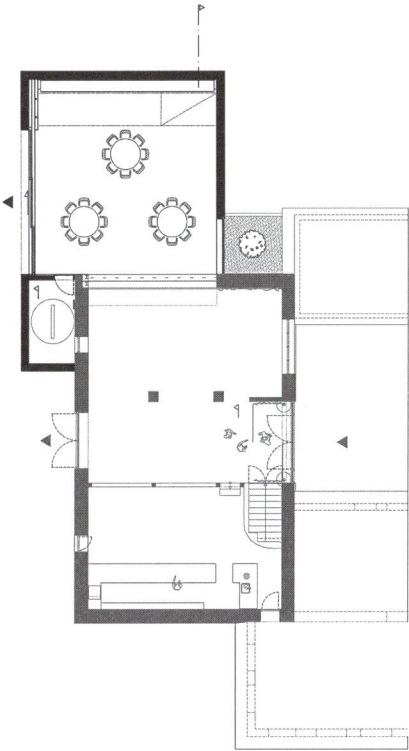

Natural lighting in extension
Extension interior
Brick mansonry and metal counter
Floor plan
Access to garden

154
PAINTING STUDIO NAGOYA JAPAN
G ARCHITECTS STUDIO
2012

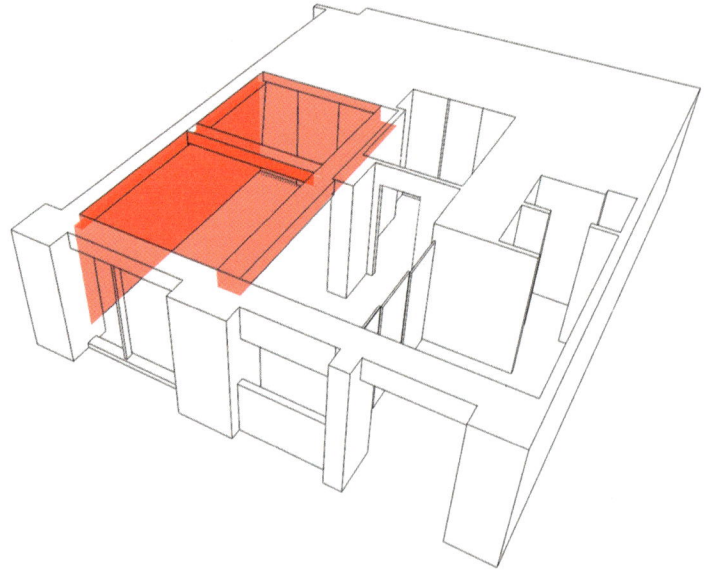

Perspective drawing
Painting Studio
Vases in front of patched reinforced concrete wall

This painting studio is a room situated in a nondescript 25-year-old apartment. The client was a painter who purchased the space as a new habitat and asked the architects to create a small studio that would also serve as a living room. During the renovation, the wallpaper was removed, revealing old, dirty concrete on the walls and ceiling. Ryohei Tanaka decided to make use of this unique texture and added a stencil design created using sheeting made of transparent resin. This material is typically used as an anti-slip surface on furniture, but was used here for masking the concrete walls.

The architect, inspired by the client's profession as an artist, employed a technique often used in painting. The white paint was sprayed on top of the stencil sheet, placed carefully on the concrete surface. The concrete wall, brought into creative harmony with the painted stencils, was thus given a lease of life. The idea behind the design was to emphasize that old is not simply old, it has a special character, like a favorite dress that has been given a new lease of life.

NOW: RYOHEI TANAKA FROM G ARCHITECTS STUDIO RENOVATED THE BUILDING AS APARTMENT AND PAINTING STUDIO. WITH A FLOOR AREA OF 60 SQUARE METERS, THE FORMER HOUSING COMPLEX IS NOW MAINLY USED FOR ARTISTIC ACTIVITIES.

PAST: THE ORIGINAL HOUSING COMPLEX WAS BUILT IN 1987, USING MAINLY CONCRETE.

Japanese decoration
Living area
Painting leaning on wall
Masking technique
Reinforced concrete wall in detail

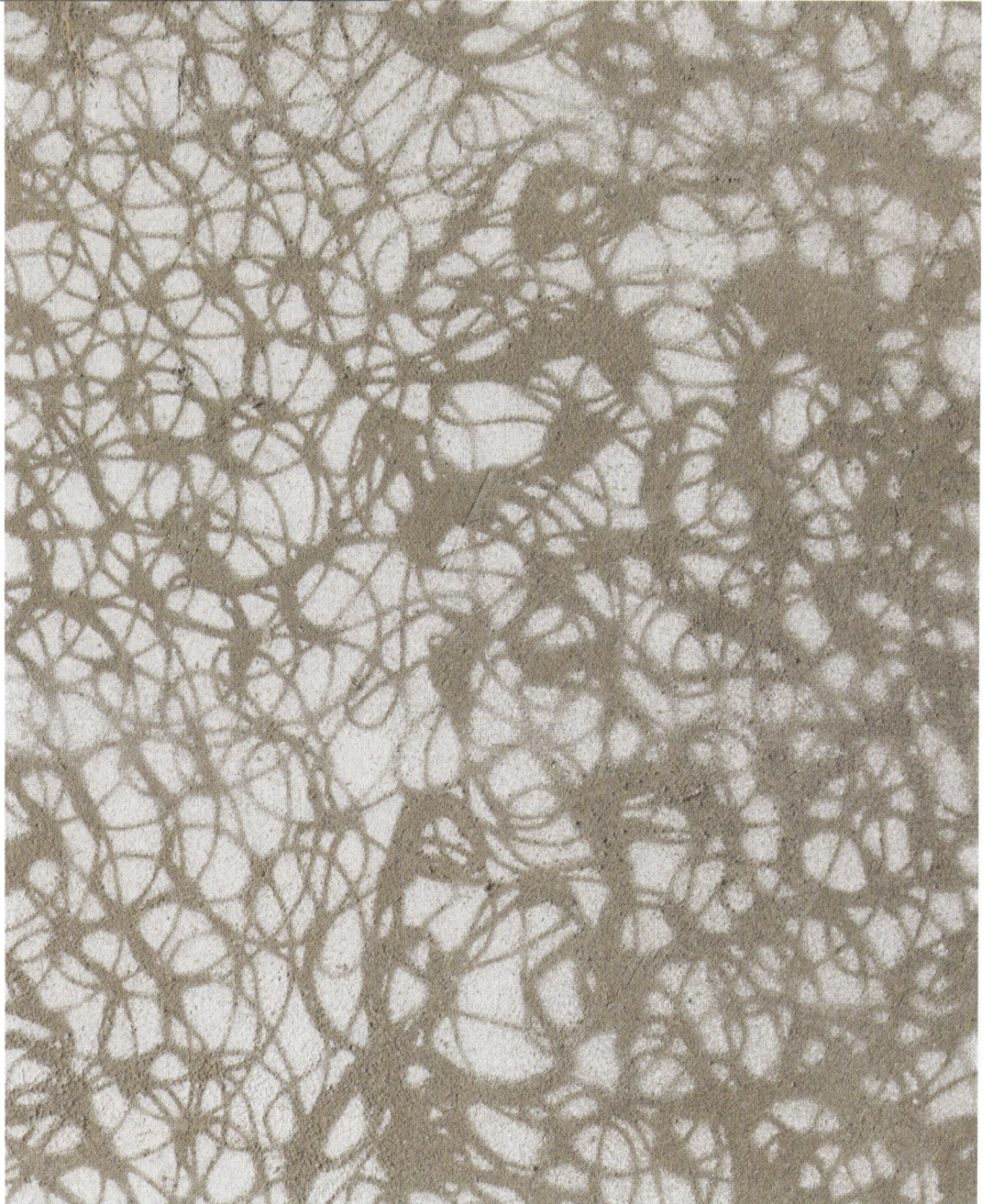

159
JHID HEAD-QUARTERS PORTLAND OR, USA
JESSICA HELGERSON INTERIOR DESIGN
2015

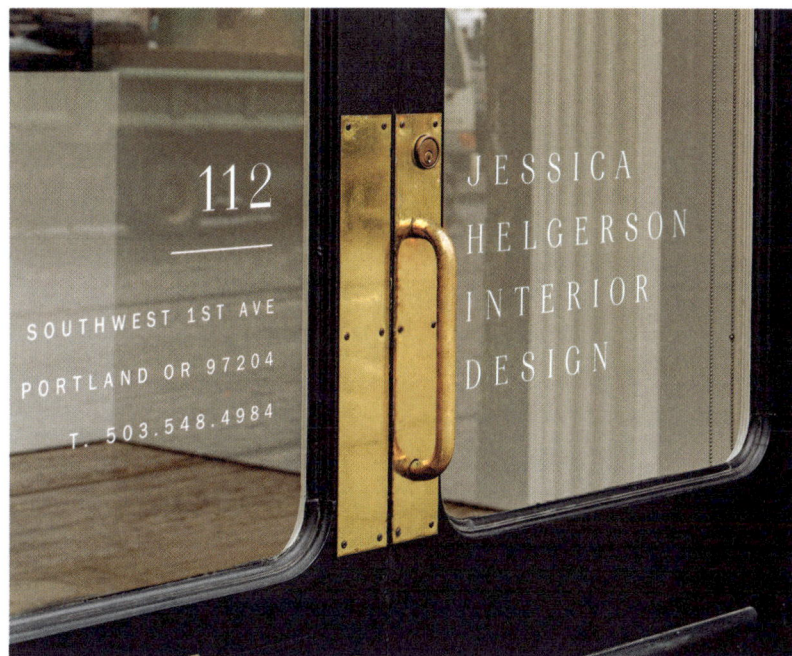

Workspace, looking to mezzanine
Front door detail

Located in downtown Portland's Old Town the office of Jessica Helgerson Interior Design is situated in the historic Railway Building, built in 1872. It features beautiful brick walls, high ceilings, a mezzanine loft conference room and huge windows facing out towards Portland's first Avenue, which is a major line of Portland's MAX light rail train. In addition to the main workspace, an expansive material library occupies the lower area under the mezzanine. Some areas of the structure have been kept in their original state, bearing the marks of decades of use, while others, such as the staircase, have been renovated.

The building was originally used for repairing trains and the machinery that was used to lift the engines still inhabits the interior. The front of the office is devoted to an installation-based art gallery called Front of House, which opened in January 2016. Here, the lower parts of the brick walls are clad with white boards.

NOW: JESSICA HELGERSON CAME UP WITH THE CONCEPT FOR THIS 206-SQUARE-METER OFFICE IN 2015, USING WOOD, PAINT AND CUSTOM-MADE FURNITURE.

PAST: THE ORIGINAL TRAIN REPAIR SHOP WAS BUILT OUT OF BRICK IN 1885.

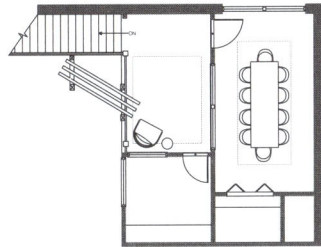

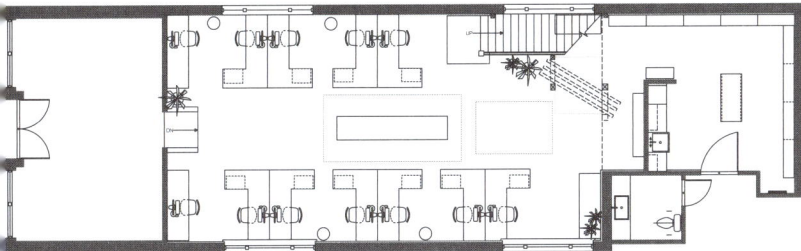

Art space called Front of House
On the mezzanine
Workspace, looking towards the front of the house
Ground and first floor plan
Elevator and stairs to mezzanine

162
STEIN HOUSE
DRUXBERGE
GERMANY
JAN RÖSLER
ARCHITEKTEN
2013

Stairs in one segment of barrel vault
View of both stories

During the renovation of this old brick barn and its transformation into a holiday home, the architects were asked to preserve the exterior look and character of the structure. Indeed, one has to look very carefully to spot the very sensitive interventions on the exterior façade.

When the wooden doors are opened, the transformed, modernized interior becomes visible. There is no disjuncture between exterior and interior. The steel girders in the Prussian-era vaulted ceiling are the dominant element in the interior. The room layout and openings are structured around the positioning of these girders. While the lower level is more suited to daytime use, the upper story comprises quieter, more intimate spaces. As far as possible, sustainable construction materials were used, for example flax insulation in the roof and loam rendering on the walls. The construction was carried out by Jan Rösler Bau and the close relationship between design and implementation thus ensured high quality and high standards at every stage of the construction process.

NOW: A PRIVATE OWNER COMMISSIONED THE ARCHITECT TO TURN THIS OLD BARN INTO A 295-SQUARE-METER HOLIDAY HOME USING BRICKS, WOOD, CLAY PLASTER AND RECYCLED OLD ROOF TILES FOR THE NEW CLADDING.

PAST: THE BARN IN SAXONY-ANHALT WAS BUILT IN THE 1930S AND CONSTRUCTED PRIMARILY USING BRICK AND WOOD, WITH CAST-IRON COLUMNS SUPPORTING THE BEAMS OF THE SEGMENTAL BARREL VAULTS.

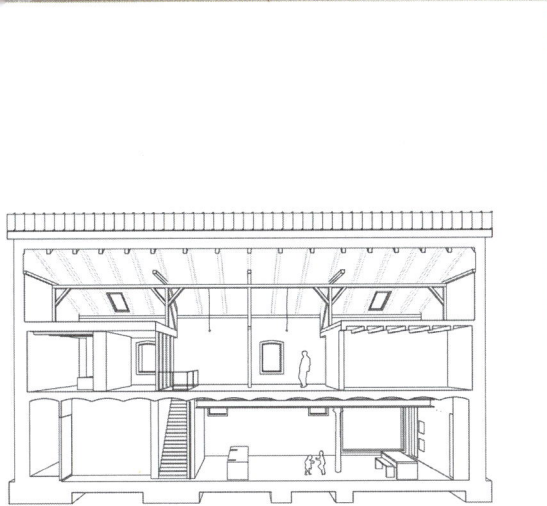

Rough Exterior
Entrance with brick walls and floor
Ground floor with cast-iron columns
Section
Clay plaster in bathroom

HOUSING RE-HABILITATION LA CERDANYA SPAIN DOM ARQUI-TECTURA 2014

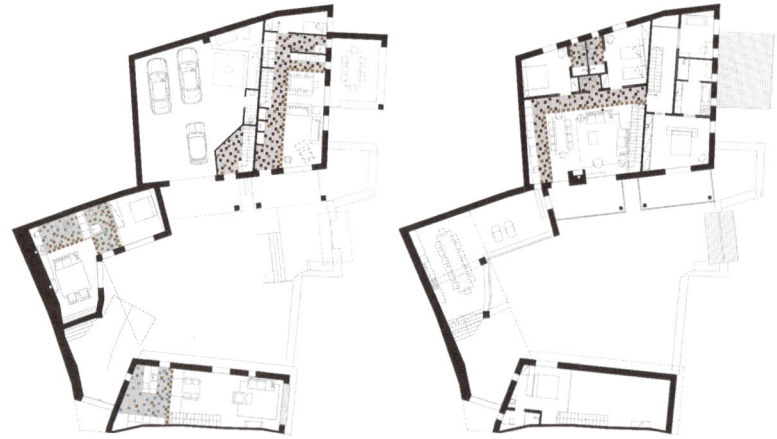

Plans
Main courtyard and Cadi Mountains
Living room
Guest house with spolium of the barn

This project is situated in a small village with breathtaking views of the Cadi Mountains. Most of the buildings in the village comprise a series of structures that surround an outdoor space called the Era. The village plan shows how the old constructions were built in order to create ensembles of living and working units arranged around enclosed spaces that are open to the elements.

In this renovation project, the size of the existing buildings was kept the same, while the façades, roofs and interior distribution have all been re-designed and adapted. The Badiu, the traditional backyard, has now become a large covered open space. The old roof trusses were used to revamp this space, which now features a vernacular roof system with no bonding material between the timber and the tiles. Inside, the rooms and guest areas retain the existing stone walls, while the flooring, tiles, woodwork and ironwork combine to create a sense of spaciousness. From many room, spectacular views can be enjoyed that seem to both blend with and flow from the interior design.

NOW: ARCHITECT PABLO SERRANO ELORDUY AND INTERIOR DESIGNER BLANCA ELORDUY COLLABORATED WITH CARLOTA DE GISPERT TO REDESIGN THIS ENSEMBLE AS 603-SQUARE-METER HOME AND GUEST HOUSE USING TRADITIONAL MATERIALS SUCH AS STONE, WOOD AND IRON.

PAST: THE ORIGINAL BUILDINGS WERE MADE OF COBBLESTONE AND WOOD, DATING BACK TO 1900. THEY FUNCTIONED AS A HAYSTACK, A BARN, A WAREHOUSE, AND A SMALL DWELLING.

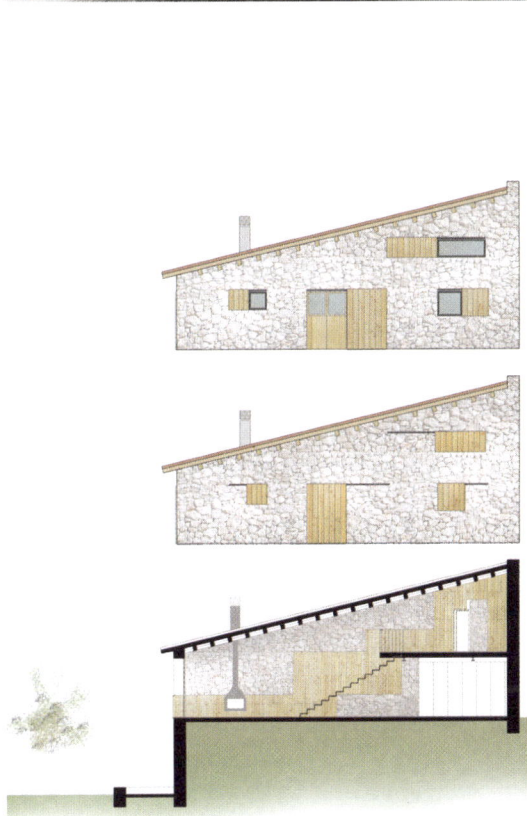

Detail of old door and new window
The former Badiu used as open space
Large window in the old structure
Elevations and section
Cobbles contrasting modern cladding

RESTAU-RANTE IXI'IM CHOCHOLÁ MEXICO

CENTRAL DE PROYECTOS JORGE BOLIO MAURICIO GALLEGOS LAVALLE + PENICHE 2016

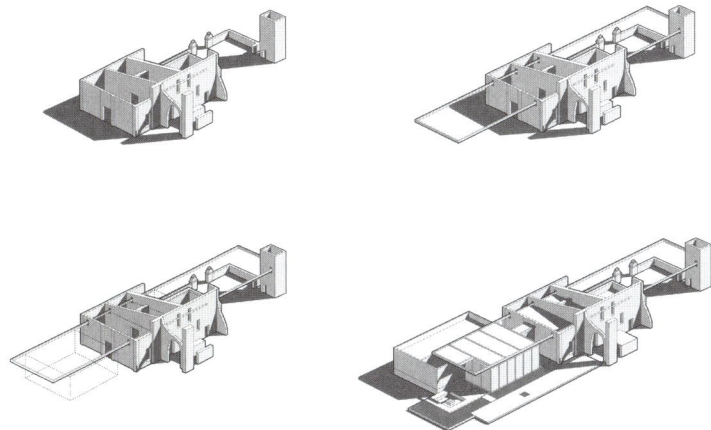

Bottles in front of glazed stone wall
Schematic drawing
Steel structure in historic setting

The Ixi'im Restaurant comprises a renovated engine house on an old henequen farm, a plant species also known as Agave fourcroydes that is native to southern Mexico and Guatemala. The new metal and glass structure has been designed to blend in with the heritage site on which it stands. The metal framework liberates the preexisting walls from structural functions, while the interior is the visual manifestation of a dialogue between heritage and intervention. Natural light is carefully filtered into the interior, enhancing the display of the largest collection of crafted liquors in the country.

Manufactured by the last active rope factory in Yucatán, the suspended henequen strings in the interior pay homage to the material in which this building has its origins, while adding to the building's acoustic qualities. The spatial sequence allows the visitor to transit between epochs, finishing in this most recent architectural addition to the site. Physically and visually integrated with the main square and its components, the space transmits a sense of respect and belonging.

NOW: SPREAD ACROSS 416 SQUARE METERS, CENTRAL DE PROYECTOS S.C.P., JORGE BOLIO ARQUITECTURA, MAURICIO GALLEGOS ARQUITECTOS, LAVALLE + PENICHE ARQUITECTOS BUILT THIS NEW RESTAURANT USING GLASS AND STEEL.

PAST: THE FORMER FACTORY WITH NATURAL STONE MASONRY WAS BUILT IN THE NINE-TEENTH CENTURY AND FELL APART IN THE SECOND HALF OF THE TWENTIETH CENTURY.

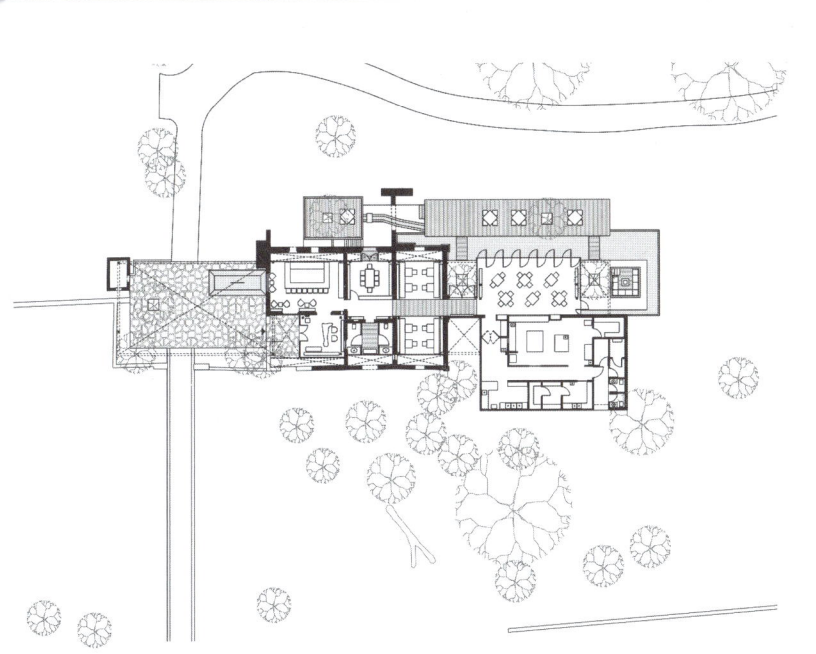

Entrance with corten steel
Restaurant panorama
Bar with liquors in front of window showing rough wall
Floor plan
Terrace between old walls

175

THE BRUNEL MUSEUM LONDON ENGLAND TATE HARMER 2016

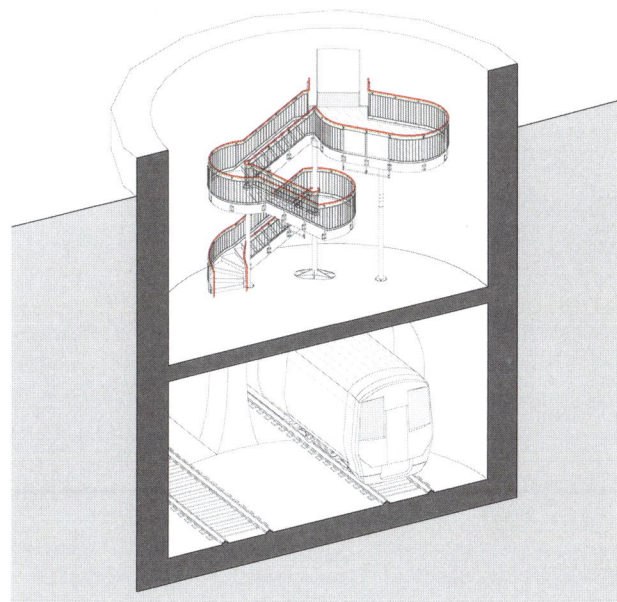

Stairs providing access
Access from Railway Avenue
Section of train tunnel

The Brunel Museum in Rotherhithe is located within Brunel's Thames Tunnel Engine House, which is a scheduled monument. Following the installation of a separating concrete deck above the tunnel, the museum has also taken a lease on the Grade II listed circular underground Sinking Shaft. This project is phase 1 of a wider masterplan for the museum, developed as collaboration between Tate Harmer and Grimshaw.

It provides access to the Sinking Shaft, with a high-level viewing platform and stairs to the lower level. This has dramatically improved visitor access to the shaft as well as providing facilities for the museum's program of performances and highlighting the beauty of the existing space. The architects used the minimum means possible in the architectural interventions, conceiving the new staircase and platform as a "ship in a bottle" structure, inserted through the new door opening and containing all the services and requirements necessary to create a working public space, whilst retaining the powerful raw atmosphere of Brunel's first structure.

NOW: TATE HARMER MADE THE SHAFT A 120-SQUARE-METER VENUE BY JUST ADDING A ELEGANT STEEL STRUCTURE WITH STAIRS AND A PLATFORM ON A NEW CONCRETE FLOOR. THE PROJECT FOR THE BRUNEL MUSEUM WAS COMPLETED IN MARCH 2016.

PAST: THE ROTHERHITHE SHAFT WAS THE ONE END OF MARC ISAMBARD BRUNEL'S THAMES TUNNEL. IT WAS MEANT AS ELEVATOR SPACE FOR HORSE-DRAWN CARRIAGES BUT USED AS CHIMNEY WHEN STEAM TRAINS RAN THROUGH THE TUNNEL.

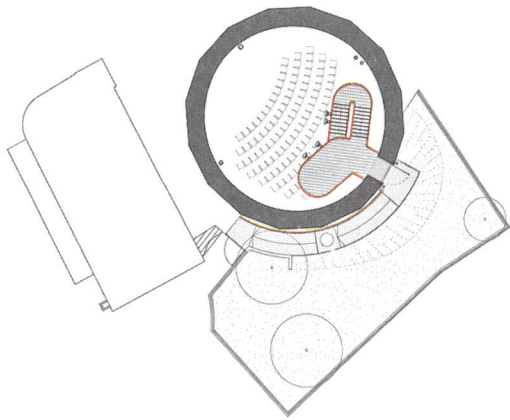

New structure with besooted walls
New structure with party taking place
Old walls and new handrail
Floor plan
Stairs with integrated lighting

TEA HOUSE HUTONG BEIJING CHINA
ARCHSTUDIO
2014

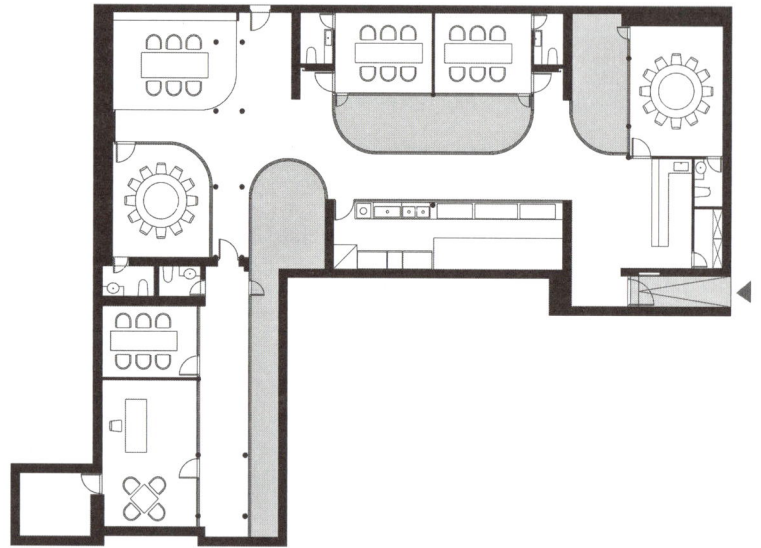

Ground floor plan with light wells
Entrance in a gap of the old structure
Table in front of historical wall

The existing building, which originally hosted company business meetings, has been transformed into a café that is sometimes used for more formal dining occasions.

The structure, wood and the particular size of the gray bricks reveal that the structure predates the Qing Dynasty. The necessary repairs were carried out with great sensitivity and respect for the historical value of the building and neighborhood. For a comfortable temperature to be maintained inside the café the structure had to be entirely enclosed. The architect Han Wenqiang also introduced a curvy corridor that creates a smooth transition from the past to the present and streamlines the building's esthetic. Light wells with Superwhite thermal bending glass provide light and divide the original courtyard to create three teahouses, each a private space with its own unique atmosphere and scenery. Warm, dark tones dominate the elements of the past, while the future enters the building as a transparent white space.

NOW: ARCHSTUDIO EXTENDED THE ORIGINAL STRUCTURE IN 2015 TO A 450-SQUARE-METER TEAHOUSE FOR A PAINTING BUSINESSMAN FROM ANHUI PROVINCE USING SUPERWHITE THERMAL BENDING GLASS, SOLID WOOD, STEEL AND CEMENT PAINT.

PAST: THE ORIGINAL BUILDING AT 25 DONGSI SHIYITIAO ALLEY IN THE DONGCHENG DISTRICT OF BEIJING DATES BACK BEFORE THE QING DYNASTY AND HAD BEEN REMODELED IN THE 1970S AND 1980S.

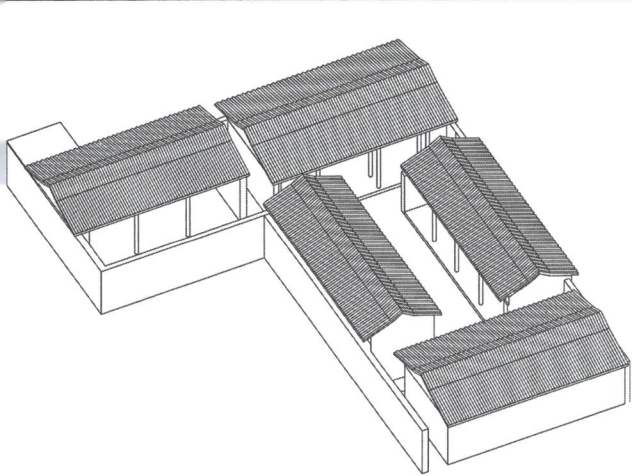

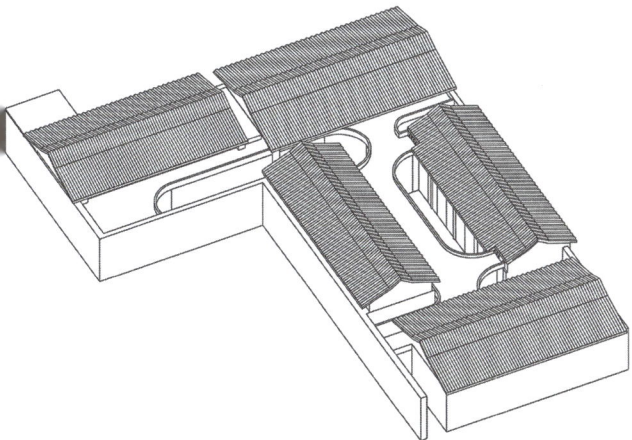

The new corridor with air wells
Contrast of historic dark and modern bright tones
Roof with new corridor and light wells
Plans of original and completed structure
New entrance

183

NANDO'S SHEPHERDS BUSH LONDON ENGLAND

STAC ARCHITECTURE 2014

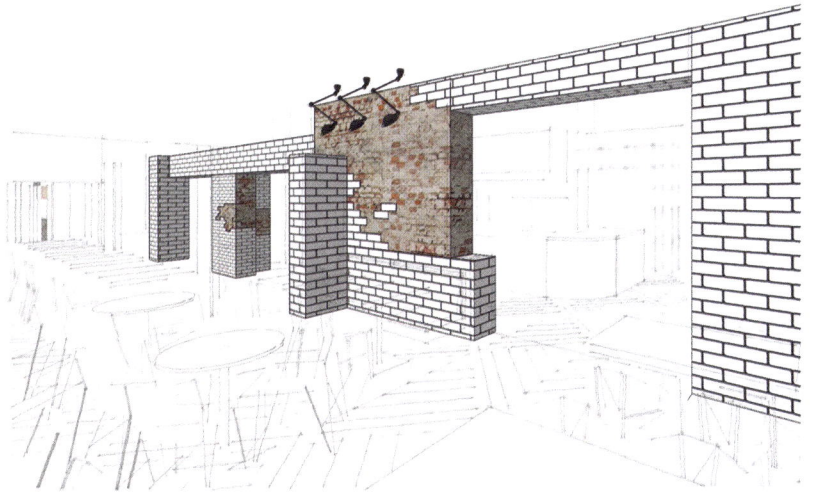

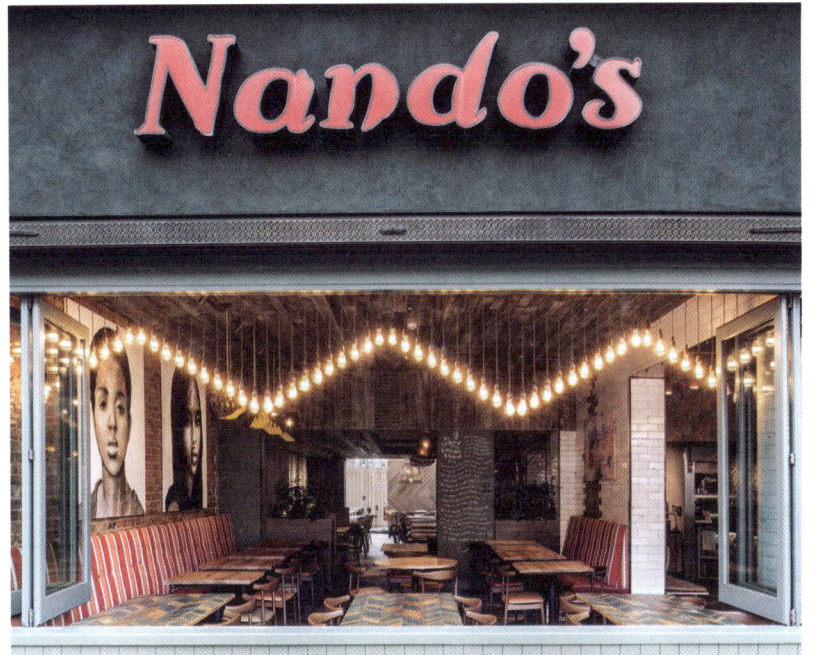

Missing glazed bricks reveal original red bricks
Sketch diagram
View from High Street into restaurant

STAC Architecture refurbished an existing tired and dark high-street restaurant. They designed the space in a way that speaks to the African heritage of the brand, whilst respecting the urban nature and location of the site.

The rear extension plays with the idea of inside and outside space whilst inviting light into the restaurant and generating the impression of al fresco dining. The existing layer of plasterboard and paneling was stripped back to reveal the original brickwork construction. One of the design challenges was to work closely with the neighbors in order to build the proposed extension directly off the original rear garden wall and use the external face of the neighboring wall within the restaurant space. The architects also restored the shop front and preserved and enhanced some of the structure's original design features. The zig-zag lighting announces the space to the street beyond and acts as a bridge between the restaurant and the city of London.

NOW: STAC ARCHITECTURE REFURBISHED THE BUILDING FOR NANDO'S UK AS HIGH STREET RESTAURANT. SPREAD ACROSS 290 SQUARE METERS, A PALETTE OF CONCRETE, OAK, PORCELAIN, LEATHER AND RECLAIMED TIMBER CLADDING HAVE BEEN USED TO CREATE A COZY AND INTIMATE SPACE.

PAST: THE ORIGINAL CONSTRUCTION OF THIS GEORGIAN TERRACE EMPLOYED TRADITIONAL MATERIALS SUCH AS LOCALLY SOURCED RED BRICK AND STONE CORBELS TO THE SHOPFRONT FAÇADE. AT STREET LEVEL, A RETAIL SPACE WAS SITUATED WITH TWO RESIDENTIAL FLOORS ABOVE.

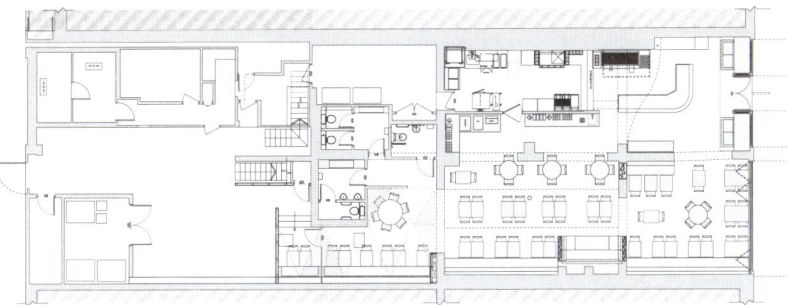

Concrete and oak tiled wall with reclaimed timber ceiling
Commissioned African art on exposed brick wall
Festoon lighting
General arrangement plan
Timber columns supporting new glazed extension

PROPERTY RECORDS HEADQUARTERS VIGO SPAIN IRISARRI-PIÑERA 2015

Section
Inner courtyard with seating area
Access route leading through inner courtyard

This project seeks to establish a balance between re-organizing the space and preserving the effect of the existing buildings. Three types of intervention were utilized and interwoven – rehabilitation, restructuring for new uses, and partial replacement, whereby certain items of value and traces of the original structure were chosen for preservation.

A courtyard organizes, connects and allows communication between different levels of the buildings. A generic and flexible spatial distribution was implemented by the architects. New and old forms of architecture meet and merge at the main entrance, which appears as a double-height space that generates a view of the courtyard from the street, forging a connection between the city and this piece of architecture. The structural typology and scale of the original buildings were largely kept the same, but the windows were modernized and thus come to symbolize the passage of time. In the courtyard, the gallery ensures the optimization of space, light and ventilation.

NOW: IRISARRI-PIÑERA RENOVATED THE ORIGINAL FOUR BUILDINGS FOR THE REGISVIGO S.L.U. AS AN OFFICE AND ARCHIVE WITH 2,979 SQUARE METERS. WHILE PRESERVING THE STRUCTURAL TYPOLOGY, THE ARCHITECTS MAINLY USED CONCRETE, WOOD AND ZINC IN THE CONVERSION.

PAST: THE ORIGINAL FOUR BUILDINGS WERE ERECTED AT DIFFERENT TIMES. THE FIRST KNOWN REFERENCE DATES FROM 1750. THE BUILDINGS WERE LIKELY USED FOR HOUSING AND BUILT USING GRANITE MASONRY AND ASHLARS.

View through large windows
Connections to different parts of the building
Interior
Office area

MISS'OPO GUEST HOUSE PORTO PORTUGAL GUSTAVO GUIMARÃES 2012

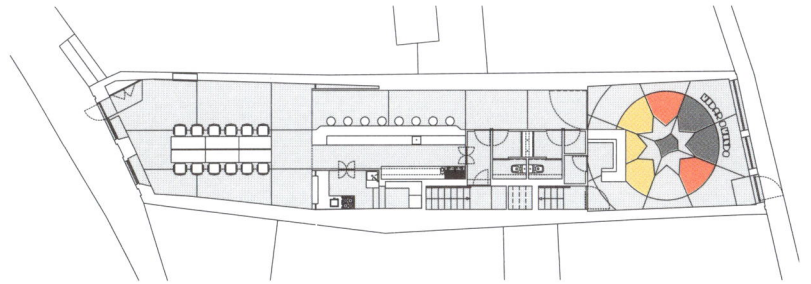

Seating area in restaurant
Floor plan
Restaurant

Miss'opo takes the ideas of intimacy and comfort and transforms these into a striking residential project. The program comprises six apartments, a restaurant space, a multi-functional space that operates as a foyer, shop and gallery, and technical areas. All of these are distributed throughout the building.

The apartments house the bedrooms, bar, kitchen, dining room and garden. The design exudes homeliness, protection and shelter and returns the building to its original function – that of a residential space. Gustavo Guimarães and his team also paid homage to the buildings more recent history, integrating its raw and industrial character as a reminder of the textile unit developed in the 1970s. A central theme of this project was to restore the building, but to respect its history, offering a new interpretation of the past. The process of conceiving and constructing Miss'opo took a total of two years.

NOW: GUSTAVO GUIMARÃES WAS RESPONSIBLE FOR CREATING THIS GUEST HOUSE AND RESTAURANT FOR MISS'OPO. SPREAD ACROSS 760 SQUARE METERS, IT WAS RENOVATED WITH CEMENT, RAW WOOD AND CONSTRUCTION BRICK TO CREATE A COZY ATMOSPHERE FOR THE GUESTS.

PAST: THE TWO ORIGINAL BUILDINGS HAD NO ARCHITECT OR PLANS. IN THE 1970S MAJOR RENOVATIONS WERE CARRIED OUT AND THE OWNER WAS ABLE TO CONNECT THE TWO EXISTING BUILDINGS TO BE USED AS A TEXTILE FACTORY. DURING THIS TRANSFORMATION, THE WOOD STRUCTURE WAS SUBSTITUTED BY CONCRETE SLABS.

In-built cupboard, and furniture
Bar
Bedroom in hotel
Hotel room with glass walls

NEUES MUSEUM BERLIN GERMANY DAVID CHIPPERFIELD ARCHITECTS JULIAN HARRAP 2009

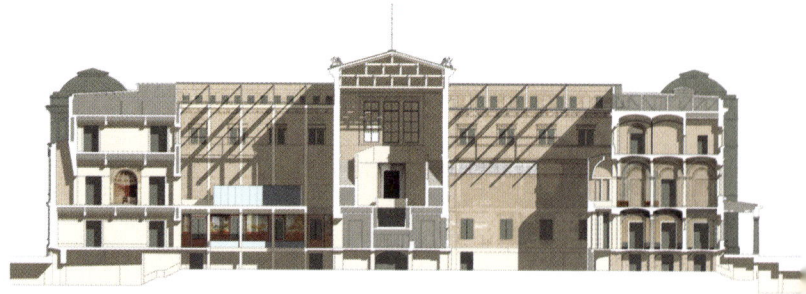

Section
View from colonnade courtyard towards Neues Museum
Staircase hall

Extensive bombing during World War II left the Neues Meuseum in ruins, with entire sections completely missing and others severely damaged. The key aim of this project was to re-complete the original volume, and involved the repair and restoration of the parts that remained after the destruction. The original sequence of rooms was restored with new building sections that create continuity with the existing structure.

The restoration and repair was driven by the notion that the original structure should be foregrounded, both in its spatial context and in its original materiality; the new reflects the lost without imitating it. The new exhibition rooms are built of large format pre-fabricated concrete elements consisting of white cement mixed with Saxonian marble chips. The north-west wing is built of recycled handmade bricks, complementing the preserved sections. After more than 60 years as a ruin, the Neues Museum reopened to the public as the third restored building on Museum Island, exhibiting the collections of the Egyptian Museum and of pre- and early history.

NOW: DAVID CHIPPERFIELD ARCHITECTS IN COLLABORATION WITH JULIAN HARRAP REFURBISHED THIS MUSEUM, WHICH WAS BOMBED DURING WORLD WAR II, FOR THE STIFTUNG PREUSSISCHER KULTURBESITZ. WITH A FLOOR AREA OF 20,500 SQUARE METERS, THE BUILDING EXHIBITS THE COLLECTIONS OF THE EGYPTIAN MUSEUM AND OF PRE- AND EARLY HISTORY.

PAST: THE ORIGINAL MUSEUM WAS BUILT ON BERLIN'S MUSEUM ISLAND BY FRIEDRICH AUGUST STÜLER BETWEEN 1841 AND 1859 FOR FREDERICK WILLIAM IV OF PRUSSIA.

Room of Niobids, view into north dome room
Egyptian courtyard
East façade Neues Museum
Greek room

198

GEOMETRY GLOBAL OFFICE HAMBURG GERMANY
PLY STUDIO
2014

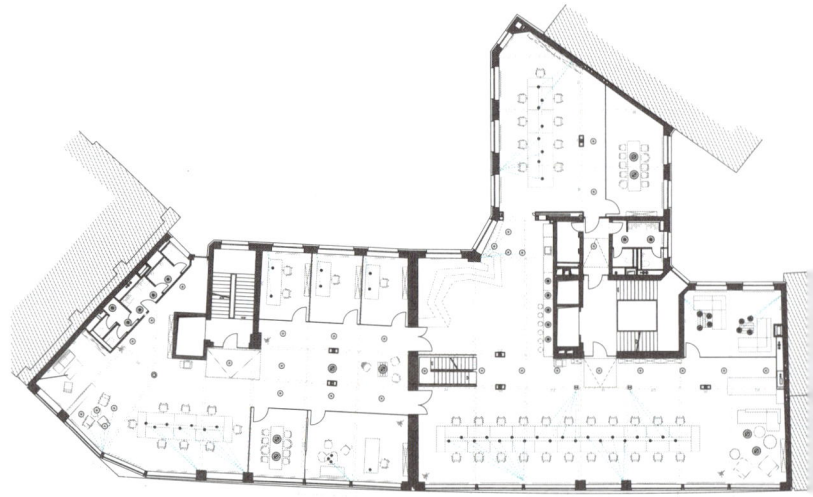

First floor plan
Kitchen area
Clocks above lounge area

This 2,000-square-meter open-space office was developed for the Hamburg branch of Geometry Global, a brand activation agency. A key focus of the design was the creation of a large open space that also offered a range of different rooms for retreat and meetings, as well as an arena, a library and a number of kitchens and lounge areas.

The design meets all the prerequisites for an open and collaborative working culture. The interior design emphasizes the agency's open-minded thinking and working principles, as well as uniting the various work disciplines. The floor planning, design, further development and implementation were carried out by PLY Studio, who were also responsible for the fixtures and fittings, characterized by esthetic contrasts. Industrial objects and lighting offset the ornamental curved windows and plaster moldings on the ceilings. A sustainable and energy-saving lighting and energy concept was implemented with the help of LEDs and lighting that is flexible in its functionality. The Kandem 831, a light developed by PLY, is a good example of this.

NOW: PLY STUDIO REDESIGNED THE BUILDING FOR GEOMETRY GLOBAL AS A NEW, INVITING OFFICE SPACE. WITH A FLOOR AREA OF 2,000 SQUARE METERS, THE BUILDING IS NOW USED AS A FLAGSHIP FOR THE DESIGN, BRANDING AND MEDIA COMPANY.

PAST: THE ORIGINAL JUGENDSTIL BUILDING WAS BUILT IN 1901 BY ALBERT LINDHORST. DECORATIVE WINDOWS AND PLASTER MOLDINGS FROM THE ORIGINAL BUILDING CAN STILL BE SEEN IN PARTS OF THE STRUCTURE.

Power points incorporated in table
Dining area with tables
Lounge area for meetings
Workspace

FASHION HUB IN FORMER MANIFATTURA TABACCHI FLORENCE ITALY STUDIO LAURIA 2016

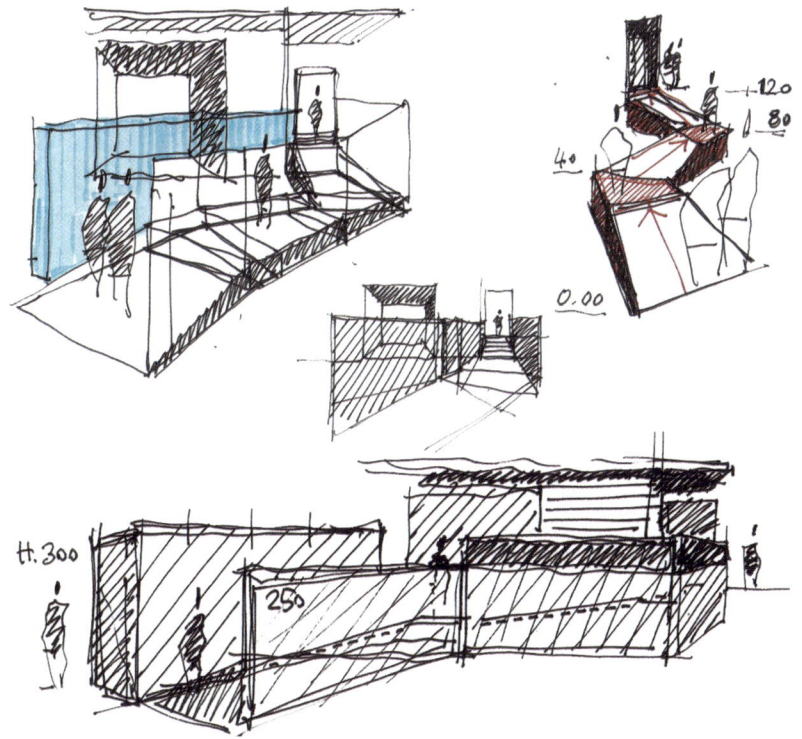

Pavilion during restoration process
Drawings of entrance ramp

Every year the event It4Fashion, organized by PIN and LogisLab, brings to Florence the major European companies working in the new technologies relevant to the fashion industry. In 2016 the event was held in the spaces of the Manifattura Tabacchi, a former tobacco factory abandoned since 2000, with the aim of reusing part of it as a temporary fashion hub.

The project seeks to combine the languages of the industrial architecture of the location with the plots and the evocative colors of the fashion technologies. The pavilions housed three conference rooms and a large exhibition hall with a tailor-made lighting design. An access ramp guiding visitors to the reception through a large entrance plaza is the visual centerpiece of the project. Twenty meters long, it is sandwiched between two wooden walls covered with iron panels in the upper part. The start of the ramp is characterized by two monolithic blocks coated with iron plates that have been burnished and slightly oxidized.

NOW: STUDIO LAURIA RE-ESTABLISHED THE BUILDING FOR PIN AND LOGISLAB MAINLY BY USING STEEL, BURNISHED IRON, WOOD AND TEXTILES. SPREAD ACROSS 5,000 SQUARE METERS, THE FORMER FACTORY IS NOW USED AS TEMPORARY FASHION HUB.

PAST: THE ORIGINAL TOBACCO FACTORY WAS BUILT BY PIERLUIGI NERVI AND GIOVANNI BARTOLI FOR THE ITALIAN GOVERNMENT BETWEEN 1933 AND 1940. REINFORCED CONCRETE, BRICKS AND MARBLE TILES WERE THE KEY MATERIALS USED TO BUILD THE FACTORY.

Start of ramp
Entrance ramp
Rear of ramp
Ramp sandwiched between wooden wall and iron blocks

ONOMICHI U2
ONOMICHI CITY
JAPAN
SUPPOSE DESIGN OFFICE
2014

Hotel reception next to common area
Guest rooms located town-like
Different functions located like shops in an urban fabric

Onomichi U2 is the result of the transformation of an old seaside warehouse into a new interactive space for Onomichi City. The redevelopment combines the charm of this town with the theme of "cycle," representing the discovery of newness in a place long established. It is a concept that has deep roots in this city. Many tourists, especially cyclists, visit Onomichi City to experience its beautiful hills and "machiya," ancient Japanese-style houses.

In 2013 the city of Onomichi accepted the architects' proposal to utilize a seaside warehouse as a new interactive space for citizens. Their plan was to completely convert the warehouse into a multi-purpose space that included a hotel, cycle shop, open areas, bars, restaurants, bakeries cafés and retail areas. All elements that were reminiscent of the character of Onomichi itself were preserved as part of the re-creation, while the wood, mortar and steel that dominate the structure evoke visual memories of the local traditions of shipbuilding and fishing.

NOW: SUPPOSE DESIGN OFFICE USED A STEEL FRAME TO CONVERT THE BUILDING TO BE REUSED AS HOTEL, SHOP, CAFÉ AND RESTAURANT ACROSS 2,697 SQUARE METERS. ARUP JAPAN HELPED THE ARCHITECTS WITH STRUCTURAL AND ENVIRONMENTAL ENGINEERING.

PAST: THE ORIGINAL STRUCTURE WAS A WAREHOUSE BUILT IN REINFORCED CONCRETE BACK IN 1943.

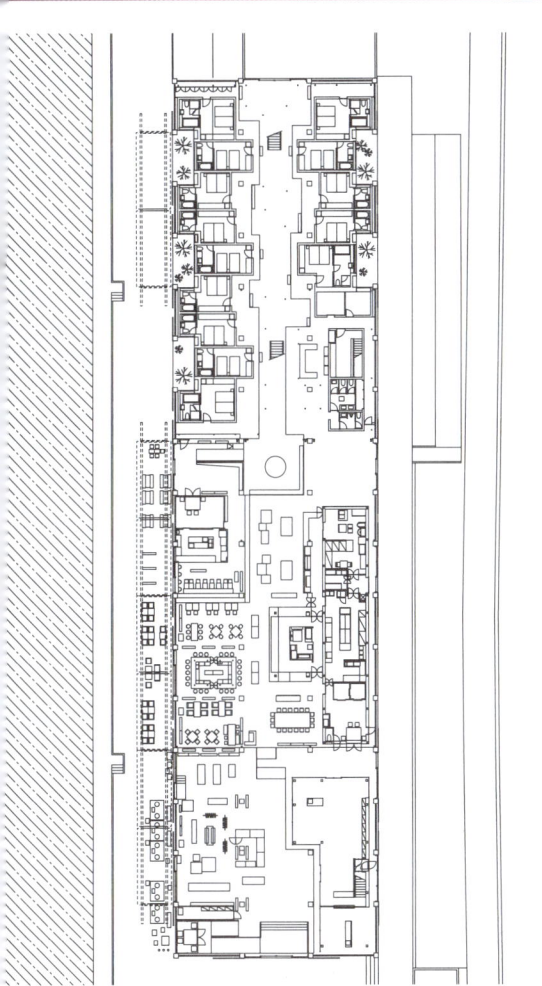

Bar with view of sea
Low bookshelves divide the space
Guests can bring their bike into hotel room
Plan
Bakery intersecting with common area to
create urban flair

211
PUBLIKUS
RESTAURANT
BUDAPEST
HUNGARY
MINUSPLUS
2014

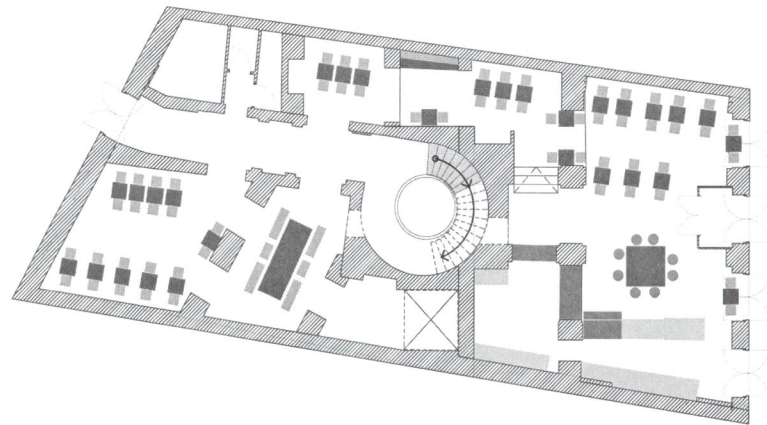

Seating area
Floor plan
Open space area

In this project, Minusplus' longtime customers, Ádám Gögge and Zoltán Horváth, the creative minds behind the soup bars Leves and Pasta, sought to channel the already well-known cozy speediness of street food into a more serious, seated restaurant atmosphere. The joint design process started out in line with this vision at the new Kecskeméti Street location in Budapest, which proved to be a bigger task in terms of the proportion of the place as well as service capacities.

Instead of sandwiches and pasta, here the hungry public of the city center can have two- or three-course meals for lunch and for dinner. The breezy, spacious and clean premises not only allow the guests to fully appreciate the architectural values of the place but, enhanced by the unique wall decorations, generate an experience that is true to the essence of Budapest.

NOW: MINUSPLUS RESTYLED THIS 350-SQUARE-METER RESTAURANT. THE SPACE WAS TRANSFORMED FOR THE PUBLIKUS ETTEREM BY ADDING NEW TILES, REMOVING PLASTER, AND DESIGNING THE RESTAURANT WITH NEW FURNITURE AND LIGHTING.

PAST: THE ORIGINAL RESIDENTIAL BUILDING WAS BUILT BY IMRE STEINDL IN 1876 USING MOSTLY STONE. LATER IT WAS USED AS A HOTEL BEFORE BECOMING A MIXED-USE BUILDING HOUSING OFFICES, RESTAURANTS AND LIVING SPACE.

Cozy dining environment
Seating area
Staircase
Lovely details on walls create a special sense of space

214

HIGHER GROUND MELBOURNE AUSTRALIA
DESIGN-OFFICE
2016

Perspectives of before and after
Chef's table
View from Platform 5

Higher Ground is an all-day dining destination on the western edge of Melbourne's business district. The former power station was re-imagined to create six new connected levels that wrap around the perimeter of the original brick building to form a suite of intimate tiered platforms.

The design approach was anchored around the creation of platforms, providing both layered perspectives and intimacy within the extensive volume of the site. The new architectural interventions are designed to sit with deliberate tension between the existing brick and concrete forms. Midnight blue staircases are expressed as confident geometric steel forms abutting the soaring columns that support the residential development above. The rich and tactile palette combines terrazzo, cork, painted steel, stone, black fiberboard and solid timbers to define and anchor each setting. Layers of planting, rugs, furniture and lighting inhabit the levels to provide a range of seating options for customers from morning to evening.

NOW: DESIGNOFFICE RE-IMAGINED THIS BUILDING FOR THE MULBERRY GROUP AS A RESTAURANT AND CAFÉ. THIS 370-SQUARE-METER FORMER INDUSTRIAL BUILDING IS NOW LINED WITH A PALETTE OF CONCRETE, CORK, METAL, STEEL AND TERRAZZO.

PAST: THE ORIGINAL BUILDING WAS BUILT BY THE MELBOURNE CITY COUNCIL ELECTRICAL SUPPLY DEPARTMENT IN 1908. THE BUILDING WAS USED FOR INDUSTRIAL PURPOSES AND WAS CHARACTERIZED BY BRICK WALLS, A TRUSSED ROOF AND ARCHED WINDOWS.

Detail of seating area and coffee bar
Ground floor dining
Furniture detail on Platform 3
Lounge area on Platform 4

219
ICONWEB HEAD-QUARTER PONTEVEDRA SPAIN
NAN ARQUITECTOS 2015

Open-plan office
Meeting room

An old billiard club, well-known in the city, has been transformed into an office for the development of digital marketing. The architects, hoping to keep the playful environment alive and to support communication and exchange among the employees, retained much of the original appearance. An open-office concept was requested from Iconweb, with a meeting room, an office, a small library, toilets and a lounge area for relaxation.

A wall made of wood and glass was inserted to contain the meeting room and the office, while desks with shared seats were introduced to encourage dialogue between employees. The lounge area was placed in a small grid near the stairs to ensure privacy. Wood and brick were the primary materials, chosen for their relationship to the original structure and for the cozy environment they generate. Hidden LEDs were placed under the seats to enhance this coziness. The overall impression is of an open space with a unique identity forged out of the conjunction of traditional and contemporary design.

NOW: THIS NEW MARKETING OFFICE WAS CREATED BY NAN ARQUITECTOS IN 2015. WITH A FLOOR AREA OF 85 SQUARE METERS, THE CONVERSION WAS DONE USING WOOD, CONCRETE AND BRICK.

PAST: THE OLD BUILDING SERVED AS A BILLIARD CLUB AND WAS ONCE A FOCAL POINT OF THE COMMUNITY.

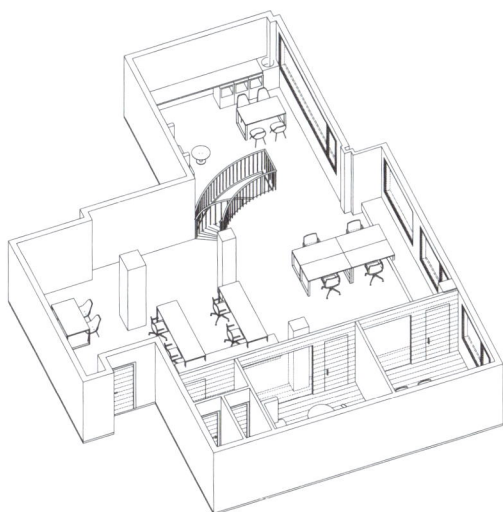

Open space
Staircase and dining area
Workspaces
Isometric diagram
Logotype

LUNE CROIS-SANTERIE
FITZROY
AUSTRALIA
STUDIO ESTETA
2015

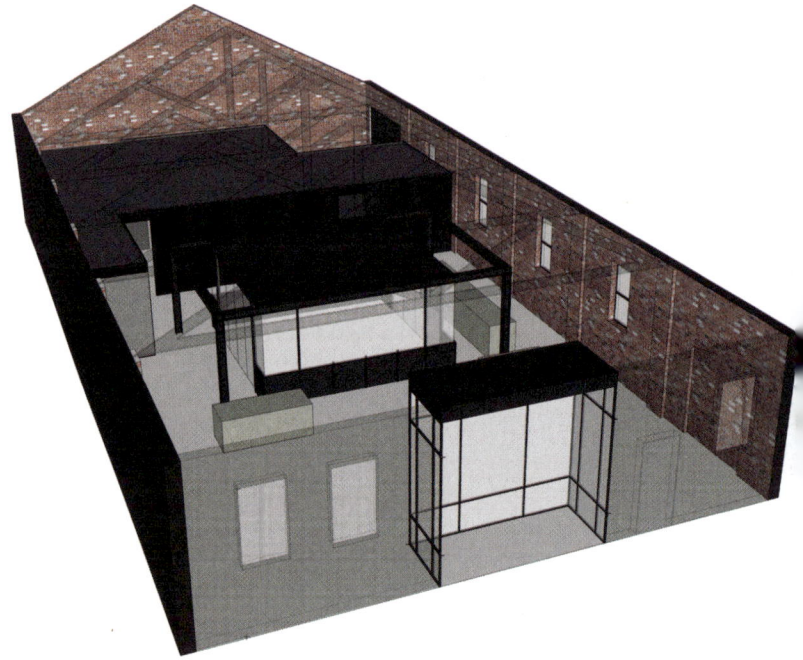

Perspective of three functional areas
Customers' view of Lune Lab
Inside Lune Lab

The client sought a design that would enable fluid and seamless production of the bakery items whilst showcasing the croissants and pastries being sold. On entering the space, the visitor first encounters the zone dedicated to bakery service. The service area is comprised of two monolithic concrete counters, with orders taken to the left, and to the right a waiting and coffee area.

This separation allows the customers to engage with the central illuminated and climate controlled glass cube, known as the Lune Lab. Dedicated to the production of the baked goods, the cube is the heart of the operation, a shrine to the pastries. Towards the rear of the space is a third area for baking and kitchen preparation. In order to remain within budget and not distract from the dynamic visual theater of the production process, the architects chose simple materials and minimized the volumetric insertions. The interior gestures were intentionally minimal and clinical. The rough and raw quality of the existing warehouse was retained, generating a contrast with the central transparent cube insertion.

NOW: STUDIO ESTETA ESTABLISHED THIS 400-SQUARE-METER CROISSANTERIE USING STEEL, CONCRETE, GLASS, PLASTERBOARD AND TILING.

PAST: BRICKWORK WAS THE MAIN MATERIAL USED WHEN THIS INDUSTRIAL BUILDING WAS ERECTED IN THE LATE NINETEENTH CENTURY.

Entry to Lune Croissanterie
Glowing show space glorifies the production process
Monolithic concrete sales counter
Glazed openings drawing attention of passersby

227

CANNON-DESIGN POWER HOUSE ST. LOUIS MO, USA CANNON-DESIGN 2008

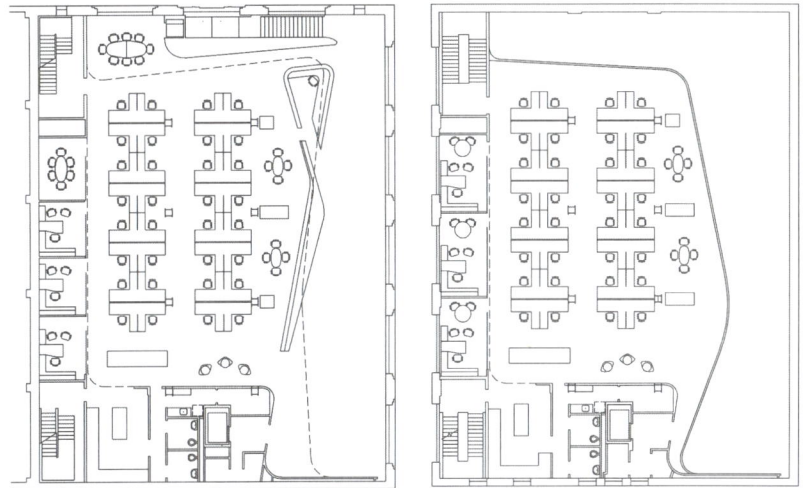

Cantilevering first and second floor
Restored historically accurate replacement of windows
Ground with first and second floor plans

After standing vacant for nearly 30 years, the St. Louis Municipal Power House building has become the new regional offices of CannonDesign. The exterior, featuring tall, arched windows on three street façades and fine terracotta detailing, has been fully restored. Although the building's exterior shell and original structural steel were fundamentally sound, reuse for a large, thriving design-focused architecture and engineering practice required a creative spatial solution that leveraged the building's massive volume in spite of its relatively small footprint.

Two new floors added within the building's massive volume accommodate continuing growth, with mezzanines preserving the arched windows on the north and east elevations and providing gallery and exhibit space for use by the firm and the larger community. They are set back from the building's spectacular windows to maintain a sense of transparency and volume. On the roof, an oblong structure, originally used to store coal conveyor equipment, now houses another boardroom and staff lunchroom.

NOW: SPREAD ACROSS 3,000 SQUARE METERS, CANNONDESIGN BUILT THEIR OWN OFFICE BY ADDING A NEW STEEL SYSTEM TO SUPPORT FIRST AND SECOND FLOOR, WHICH CANTILEVER OUT INTO THE GROUND FLOOR GALLERY.

PAST: THE POWER HOUSE WAS AN ORIGINAL PART OF THE MUNICIPAL SERVICE BUILDING COMPLEX. MAINLY BRICK AND CONCRETE WERE USED TO BUILD THE WAREHOUSE IN 1928. IT WAS DECOMMISSIONED BY THE CITY IN 1980.

Two separate floor plates floating inside the tall volume
Restored windows provide daylight and transparency
New structure inside designated national landmark
Boardroom and staff lunchroom on the roof

231

POSABILE
PERUGIA
ITALY

SPECIAL-UMBRIA
2015

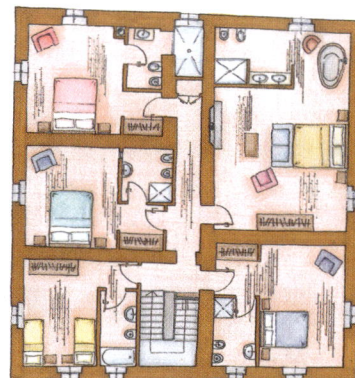

Piano Primo

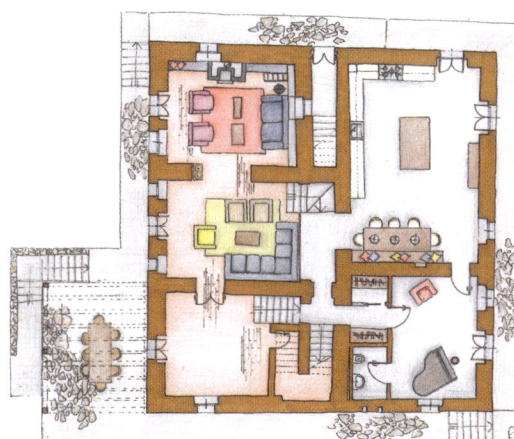

Piano Terra

Cozy couch corner with fireplace
First floor plan
Ground floor plan

The aim for this beautiful old farmhouse was to create a child-friendly house whilst retaining and celebrating its unique Umbrian style. A new opening between the revamped kitchen and lower stables was created due to a significant difference in floor level and the living areas have been connected to the cooking and dining space.

The old internal stairs were removed and on the opposite side of the house a large new internal staircase was created. All original materials found in and around the house were reused where possible. The old shutters were brought back to life as kitchen doors, bedside tables and coffee tables, while the doors became bed stands. The original front doors were redeployed as the linen cupboard. The floors in the house perfectly demonstrate how modern and classic can sit comfortably side by side, with traditional handmade cotton floors on the upper level and in the living areas and a modern resin floor in the kitchen and hall. The living room with its enormous fireplace has been turned into an open-plan master bedroom and open bathroom.

NOW: SPECIALUMBRIA IN COOPERATION WITH SPR TAVERNELLE RESTORED THIS BUILDING AS RENTAL HOLIDAY HOME FOR GROUPS UP TO 12 PEOPLE. SPREAD ACROSS 450 SQUARE METERS, THE ORIGINAL FARMHOUSE NOW SERVES AS COMFORTABLE ACCOMMODATION.

PAST: THE TRADITIONAL ITALIAN FARMHOUSE WAS BUILT IN THE SIXTEENTH CENTURY. MAINLY BRICK, LOCAL ROCK STONE AND COTTO (BAKED CLAY) WERE USED DURING THE CONSTRUCTION.

Piano in front of brick wall
New staircase with glass landing above bread oven and
original front doors on wall
Bed beneath sloping wooden ceiling
Freestanding copper bathtub

BED&BUNKER TALE ALBANIA
UNIVERSITY OF MAINZ – INTERIOR DESIGN 2012

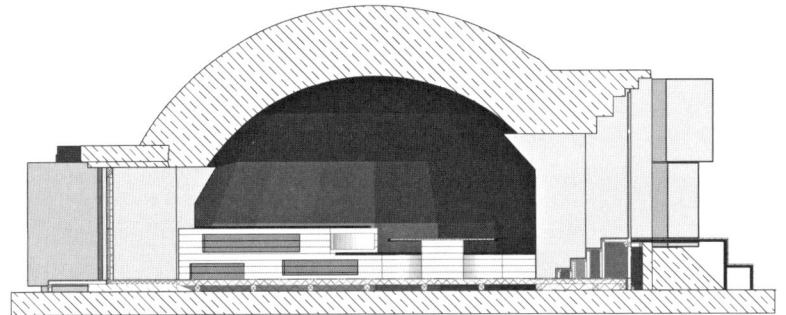

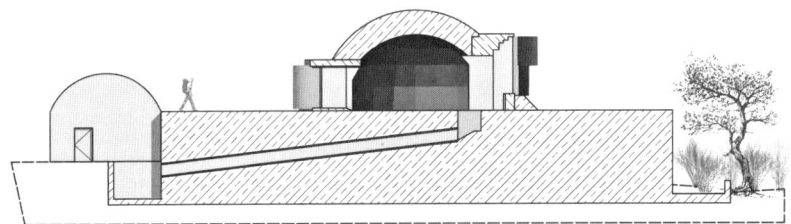

Exterior view at sunset
Interior space
Section of storage space
Section of platform

This project, based on the diploma thesis of Iva Shtrepi, was conceived as an attempt to understand abandoned bunkers as an architectural resource. The project team – students and teachers of the University of Applied Sciences Mainz and Polis University of Tirana – supervised by Markus Pretnar, Franziska Mamitzsch, Endrit Marku and Endrit Barjami converted one bunker into a minimalist hostel for individual tourists as a low-cost, do-it-yourself construction. Bed&Bunkers is one of approximately 400,000 bunkers in Albania. The dome has a thickness of 1.3 meters, which ensures natural cooling during the hot months and heat storage in winter. A door was fitted at the entrance to the bunker and the former gun slit became a large window.

The first major decision taken in the design process was to execute the interior work in wood. All inner walls of the dome were kept in the original gray concrete. Esthetic diversity was a fundamental concept in this project and was partly realized by the creation of various relaxing "islands" of different heights. The kitchen provides space for sitting as well as a sink, a gas stove, and a small fridge.

NOW: THE UNIVERSITY OF MAINZ IN COOPERATION WITH POLIS UNIVERSITY IN TIRANA CONVERTED THE FORMER GUN BUNKER INTO AN ACCOMMODATION FOR INDIVIDUAL TOURISTS. SPREAD ACROSS 56 SQUARE METERS, MAINLY SOLIC STRUCTURAL TIMBER, SQUARE TIMBERS, BOARDS, PANEL MATERIAL, AND TILES WERE USED.

PAST: THE ORIGINAL GUN BUNKER WAS BUILT BETWEEN 1972 AND 1984 DURING THE REIGN OF ENVER HOXHA. THE MAIN MATERIALS FOR THE CONSTRUCTION OF THIS GUN BUNKER OF TYPE M45 (CLIFFSIDE BUNKER) WERE CONCRETE SLABS, WHICH WERE INSERTED INTO A WALL OF 130 CENTIMETER DEPTH.

View from kitchen in direction of terrace
Seating and relaxation landscape and kitchenette
View from terrace in direction of entrance
View from kitchen in direction of terrace

238
LOFT
KREUZBERG
BERLIN
GERMANY
MEYLENSTEIN
2014

Stairs in front of bricks
Cooking and dining area
Kitchenette

During renovation work, great importance was attached to preserving the loft-like character of the space. The charm of the original was preserved and enhanced by the addition of new, clear-cut forms. One of these was a concrete cube, positioned at the heart of the structure. Two concrete staircases lead to an open sleeping area with large bath in the upper story, while each of the cube's surfaces is finished with a layer of concrete.

In contrast to the open space on the upper level, a small room is concealed behind a hidden door, the existence of which is betrayed only by a two-millimeter joint. The kitchen-dining area is dominated esthetically by a solid in-situ concrete island. A mobile countertop on wheels allows for flexible use of the kitchen space. Blue Boxes are positioned just under the roof and arranged in a staggered geometrical formation. A continuous line of lights passing along the back edge of the Blue Boxes functions as an accentuating feature, drawing one's gaze towards the open space beyond the boxes and the pitched roof above. In the living room, uplights work to emphasize the textures in the untreated brick walls.

NOW: MEYLENSTEIN RENOVATED THIS BUILDING TO CREATE A COMFORTABLE HOME BY MAINLY MAINTAINING EXISTING WOOD AND ADDING CONCRETE AS WELL AS DRY LINING. BOASTING AN AREA OF 240 SQUARE METERS, IT IS NOW USED AS A PRIVATE HOME.

PAST: THE ORIGINAL RESIDENTIAL BUILDING WAS BUILT IN AROUND 1910. IT WAS CONSTRUCTED MAINLY USING MASONRY AND WOOD.

Concrete cube
Living area
Bedroom with large bath
Floor plan
Blue Boxes containing bathroom, dressing room and
guest room

243

TEGOYO I
LANZAROTE
SPAIN
NÉSTOR
PÉREZ
BATISTA
2014

Exterior
Window seat
Interior design

The surrounding landscape was the project's primary feature and one of the main challenges was therefore to establish a very close and vital relationship between the natural and the architectural elements. This project is located in La Geria and combines a residential program with agricultural activity.

The clients required two suites, divided into two main areas: sleeping and living. Each space is devised individually but is connected strategically to its neighbors and to the countryside spaces, creating a harmonious whole. The detailed attention to aspects such as lighting, spatial geometry, ambient comfort and privacy allows the unit to be experienced as a unified structure, while also providing a variety of conditions and spatially differentiated characteristics. Apertures emphasize the feeling of transparency and ensure that the spatial continuity is undisturbed. The natural materials of the existing stable and warehouse – stone, wood, clay, cement, limestone and glass – and the traditional architecture of the island were chosen for this intervention.

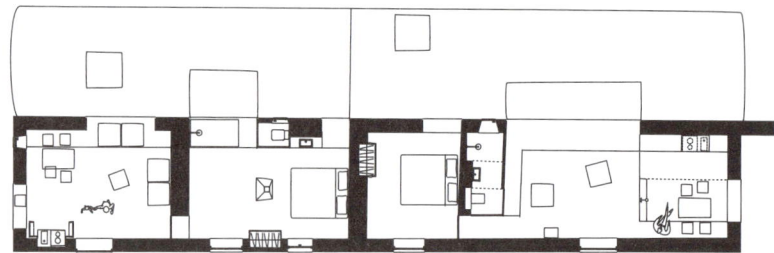

NOW: NÉSTOR PÉREZ BATISTA ADAPTED THE BUILDING AS A FUTURE RESIDENCE FOR FAMILY BETHENCOURT. SPREAD ACROSS 130 SQUARE METERS, THE ORIGINAL BUILDING WAS TRANSFORMED WITH GLASS, CEMENT, STONE, WOOD AND CLAY.

PAST: THE ORIGINAL AGRICULTURAL STORAGE WAS BUILT IN THE EIGHTEENTH CENTURY.

Large openings give the building a friendly appearance
Ground floor plan
Living room
Site plan
Lounge area

CANAL FACTORY RE-HABILITATION PALENCIA SPAIN

ADAM BRESNICK ARCHITECTS JOSÉ ANTONIO SALVADOR POLO

2015

Dining room
Factory logo

The Canal Factory is located near the Canal of Castile and is registered as a cultural heritage site. Composed of volumes built at different times, the thick walls envelop a three-story pine assemblage of pillars, beams and floor slabs. The intervention involved the installation of a restaurant on the ground floor; the first phase in a comprehensive project including spa, hotel and exterior recreational areas. This project makes ideal use of the building, given its privileged location alongside a wide docking area and its easy access to the canal towpath.

The area with machinery has been converted into a museum and dining room; so that the culinary experience is accompanied by the old machines. The new uses have been articulated with maximum respect for the buildings' past: resolving building pathologies ranging from leaking roofs to problems with wood decay and pests. The wood structure has been reinforced where necessary, doubling joists to meet current building code, yet always facilitating the reading of old and new elements.

NOW: THIS REGISTERED CULTURAL HERITAGE SITE WAS TRANSFORMED INTO A RESTAURANT AND MUSEUM.

PAST: THE ORIGINAL FLOUR MILL AND WAREHOUSE BUILDING WAS BUILT IN 1854 AND WAS USED AS SUCH UNTIL 1979. FROM 1994 UNTIL 2002 IT WAS USED AS A CENTER OF CONTEMPORARY ART. IT IS CHARACTERIZED BY BRICK WALLS AND WOODEN BEAMS.

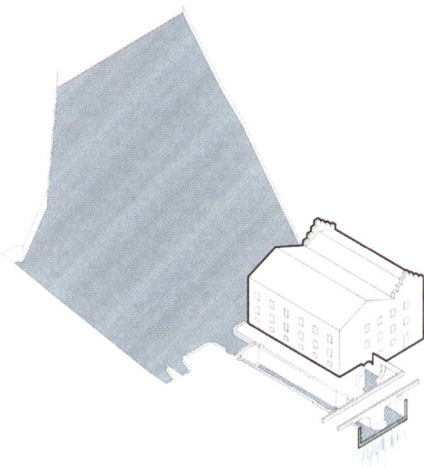

Seating area beside bar
Bar
Table in restaurant
Plan
Exterior view

NEUE WEST
BERLIN
GERMANY
ARNKE
HÄNTSCH
MATTMÜLLER
AHM
ARCHITEKTEN
2016

Site plan
Exterior view
New and light-flooded attic in the factory

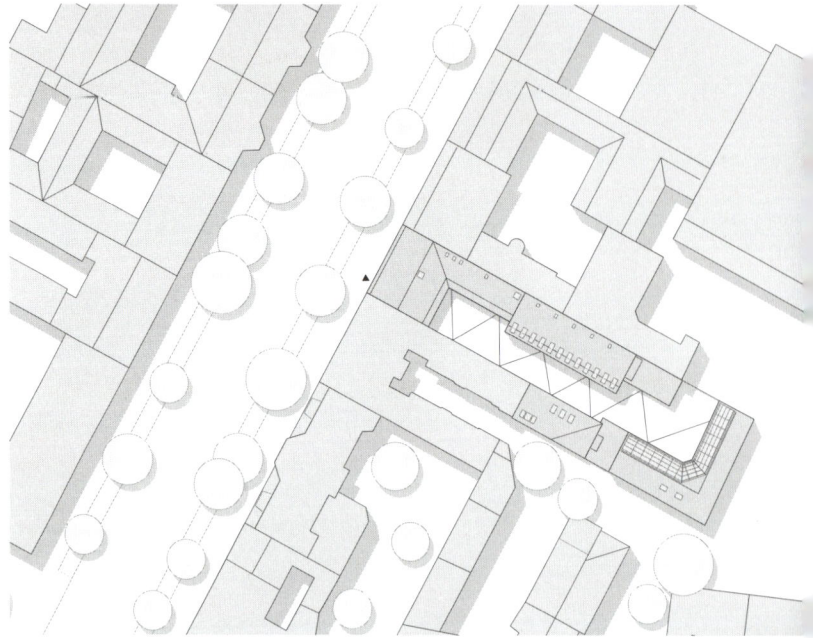

The Neue West building ensemble comprises four structures connected by a long internal courtyard. The building, located directly adjacent to Potsdamer Straße, features a passageway and forms the entrance to the ensemble. A second structure and a villa lead, via a kind of alleyway, into the heart of the site, which is dominated by the L-shaped factory building.

The aim of the restoration was to preserve as much as possible of the existing structure and its artisan qualities. The existing roof framework had to be removed and replaced due to severe damage. As a result, each of the four structures was given a new, expansive attic story. In the building positioned at the front of the site, the existing floor coverings could be preserved and repaired, while in the other buildings the floor coverings were replaced. Renovated, contemporary elements merge with relics of the past to create an architecturally harmonious impression. The restructuring of the ensemble, undertaken to comply with conservation guidelines, generates a space that can be used in countless, creative ways.

NOW: AHM ARCHITEKTEN RENOVATED THE 5,400-SQUARE-METER ENSEMBLE OF BUILD-INGS FOR ANH HAUSBESITZ FROM 2014 TO 2016. THE BUILDINGS WERE RESTORED USING CONCRETE, BRICKWORK, WOOD, GLASS AND STEEL AND NOW ACCOMMODATE OFFICE SPACE AND GASTRONOMIC ENTERPRISES.

PAST: THE ORIGINAL BUILDINGS WERE CONSTRUCTED BETWEEN 1840 AND 1880 USING BRICK AND WOOD. THEY WERE USED FOR RESIDENTIAL AND BUSINESS PURPOSES.

Attic inside building
Attic in villa
Special ceiling structure and light in passage
Old wall structure in front building

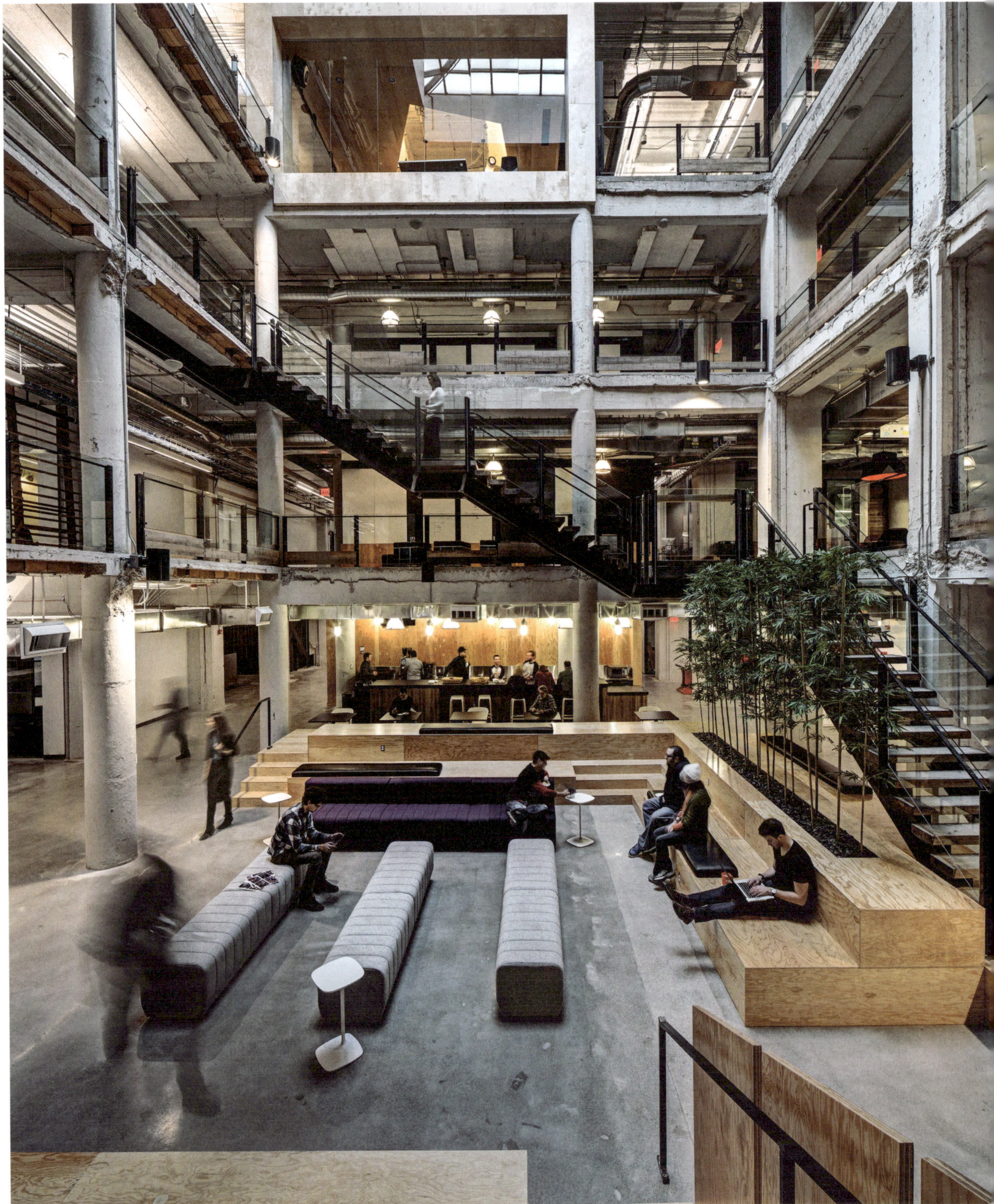

255

CAMPBELL EWALD DETROIT MI, USA
MCINTOSH PORIS ASSOCIATES
2014

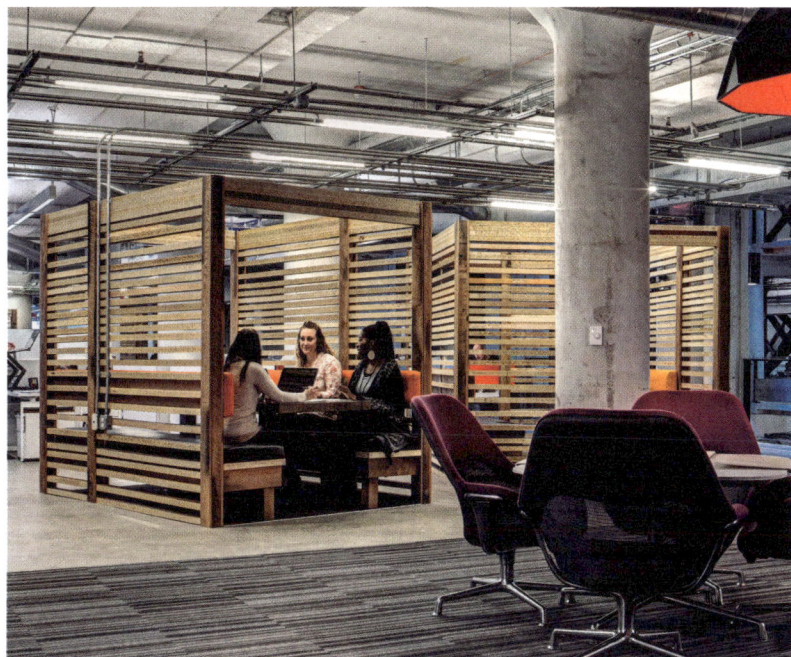

Lobby-level atrium designed as workplace and social hub
Break-out spaces define informal work and meeting areas

The office of Campbell Ewald, a national advertising and marketing communications agency, was designed by McIntosh Poris Associates to reflect the company's identity, values and character. Set in a former Hudson's Department Store warehouse, the office promotes spontaneous interaction among departments to foster both creative collaboration and independent work.

Given the nature of the building, the design enlarges definitions of workspace by mixing old and new, as well as industrial and modern sensibilities, with a palette of concrete, steel and wood. The design offers a simple, cost-effective solution resulting in an active, collaborative environment. The lobby-level atrium acts as the social hub. Bench seating, plantings, coffee bar, and bleachers offer views of the activity in the offices and meeting rooms above. Existing large windows and newly installed skylights create a glow in the space for both large and small gatherings. Break-out spaces dispersed throughout the floor plan offer focused work zones and outlets for impromptu meetings and creative encounters.

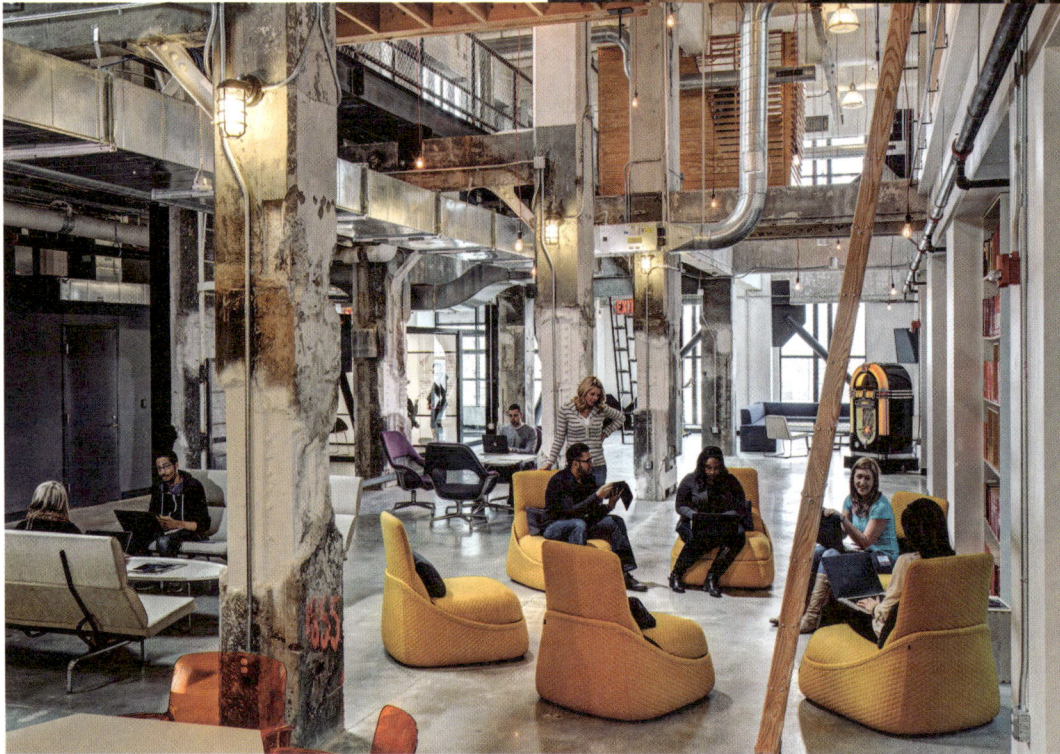

NOW: MCINTOSH PORIS ASSOCIATES DESIGNED THE ADVERTISING OFFICE FOR CAMPBELL EWALD AS A MODERN AND PLEASANT 11,300-SQUARE-METER WORKSPACE. CONCRETE, METAL AND WOOD WERE THE DOMINANT MATERIALS CHOSEN BY THE ARCHITECTS.

PAST: THE ORIGINAL WAREHOUSE WAS CONSTRUCTED FOR HUDSON'S DEPARTMENT STORE IN 1911 BY THE ARCHITECTS SMITH, HINCHMAN AND GRYLLS.

A coffee bar offers seating for casual breaks and meetings
Office spaces foster collaboration and independent work
New skylights draw natural light into office spaces
Third floor plan
Interiors mix industrial and modern sensibilities

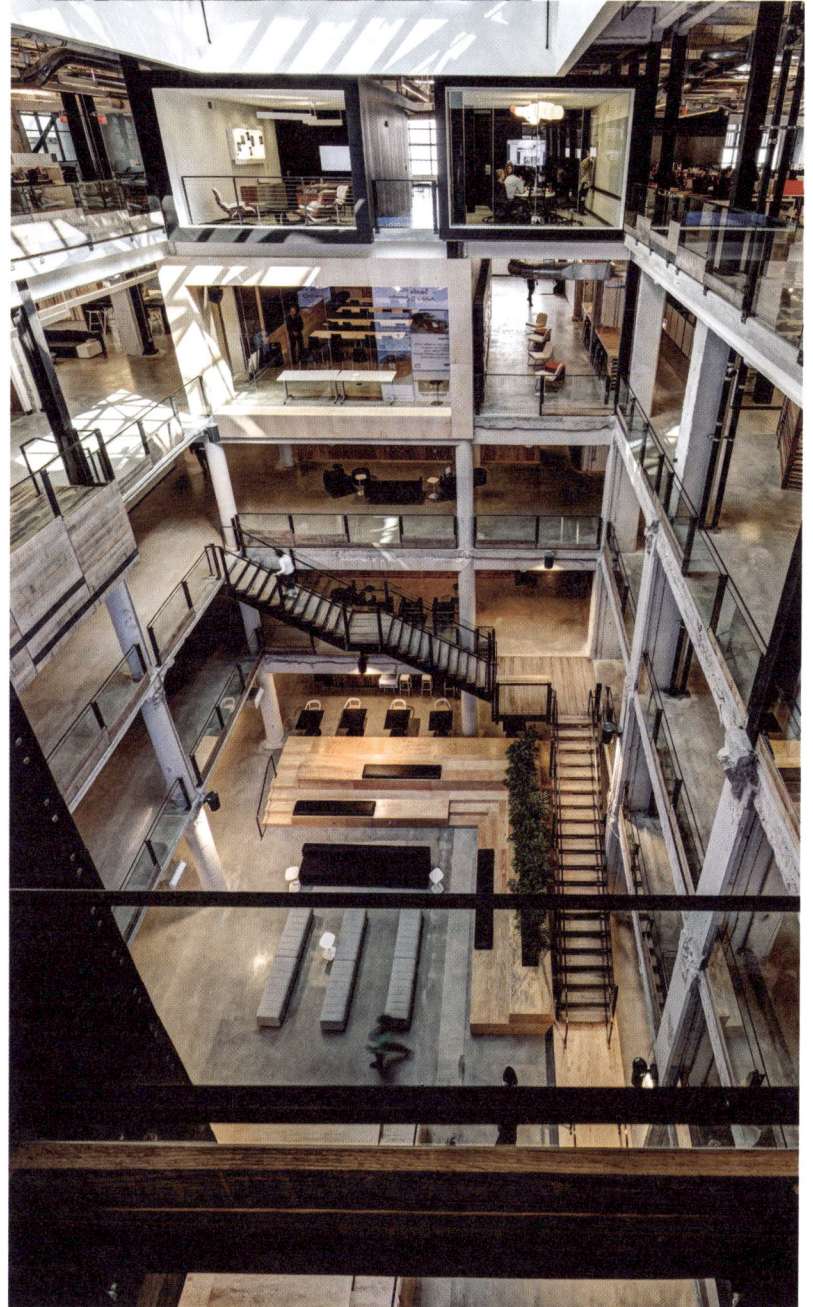

DCA STUDIO
NEW DELHI
INDIA
GROUP DCA
2012

Ground floor plan
Reception in the evening
Box-in-box design principle creates private space

Designed as a studio space for an architecture and interior design firm within an existing warehouse, the main challenge was to retain as much of the original structure as possible, while retrofitting the interior to meet the stringent parameters laid out in the design brief.

The space was to be naturally lit as far as possible and needed to provide a naturally ventilated and flexible workspace for a growing team of design professionals. Additionally, the studio needed to foster a high level of interaction between the studio and the project team. Conceived as a box-in-box, the office provides engaging spaces for both private and communal use, fostering a sense of creative continuity, allowing spaces for both brainstorming and focused work. A combination of old and new furniture, along with elegantly detailed new lighting helps to create the desired ambience. The design successfully employs a complex layering of spatial hierarchies that caters to the flexibility essential for a growing design services firm.

NOW: GROUP DCA RESTORED THIS BUILDING TO SERVE AS THEIR COMPANY OFFICE. SPREAD ACROSS 370 SQUARE METERS, THE TRANSFORMATION WAS ACHIEVED USING KOTA FLOORING, EXPOSED BRICKWORK, VINYL FLOORING AND RUBBER WOOD.

PAST: MAINLY BRICK AND MORTAR WERE USED TO BUILD THE ORIGINAL WAREHOUSE.

Work table in front of bookshelf
Work tables for individual or group work
Reception
Individual work spaces

263

RUIN ACADEMY TAIPEI TAIWAN CASAGRANDE LABORATORY 2010

Interior view
Exterior view

The Ruin Academy occupies an abandoned five-story apartment building in central Taipei. It organizes workshops and courses for Taiwanese people and international guests. The building does not rely purely on design, but instead has an intimate relationship with the broader environment of the Taipei basin and can be understood as a response to this environment. As a tangible element in this relationship, the façades were penetrated with six-inch holes in order to let rain inside the building. In the future, the academy hopes to become involved in urban farming and thus contribute towards the city's embrace of the organic idea.

The driving force behind this project was to rethink both the industrial city and our modern existence as urban beings. A key principle was that architecture should be free to embrace both environmental art and urban design.

NOW: CASAGRANDE LABORATORY RE-ESTABLISHED THE BUILDING FOR THE JUT FOUNDATION OF ARTS & ARCHITECTURE AS AN EDUCATIONAL ACADEMY. WITH AN AREA OF 500 SQUARE METERS THE RUIN ACADEMY HAS BEEN TRANSFORMED USING WOOD, WATER, CONCRETE AND BRICK.

PAST: THE ORIGINAL BUILDING WAS USED AS AN APARTMENT BUILDING AND WAS COMPRISED MAINLY OF CONCRETE.

Living area
Bathroom
Sauna
Second floor plan
Wooden wall and floor

267

ASHTON OLD BATHS TAMESIDE ENGLAND
MCAU
2017

View from existing first floor gallery
Gable end of the new structure

The new vision for this former municipal swimming bath was to bring the building back into use as a creative, digital and media hub. The project was split into two separate phases. Phase one included the complete restoration of the former main pool hall and the entire building's exterior, as well as the introduction of 650 square meters of modern office space in the form of an independent freestanding structure.

Phase two will involve the restoration and fit-out of the adjacent annex. Early in the design process, the viability of installing new office space into the main pool hall was considered and due to its listed status the concept of a building within a building was taken forward. The new offices would be independent from the existing structure, to simplify the structural solution, but more importantly to maintain the integrity of the existing building's internal fabric. The new, freestanding structure provides new workspace units with additional meeting rooms, breakout areas, and a new rooftop communal terrace. The exterior of the building has been completely restored and refurbished.

NOW: MCAU CONVERTED THE ORIGINAL BATH INTO AN OFFICE FOR PLACEFIRST LTD/ TAMESIDE MBC, USING A STEEL FRAME WITH PLYWOOD AND WESTERN RED CEDAR CLADDING, DOUBLE-GLAZED SCREENS AND DRY LINED PAINTED INTERNAL WALLS.

PAST: ASHTON OLD BATHS WAS BUILT IN THE 1870S FOR TAMESIDE COUNCIL. DESIGNED BY ARCHITECTS PAULL AND ROBINSON IN THE ITALIANATE ROMANESQUE STYLE, IT BECAME THE BEATING HEART OF A THRIVING COMMUNITY.

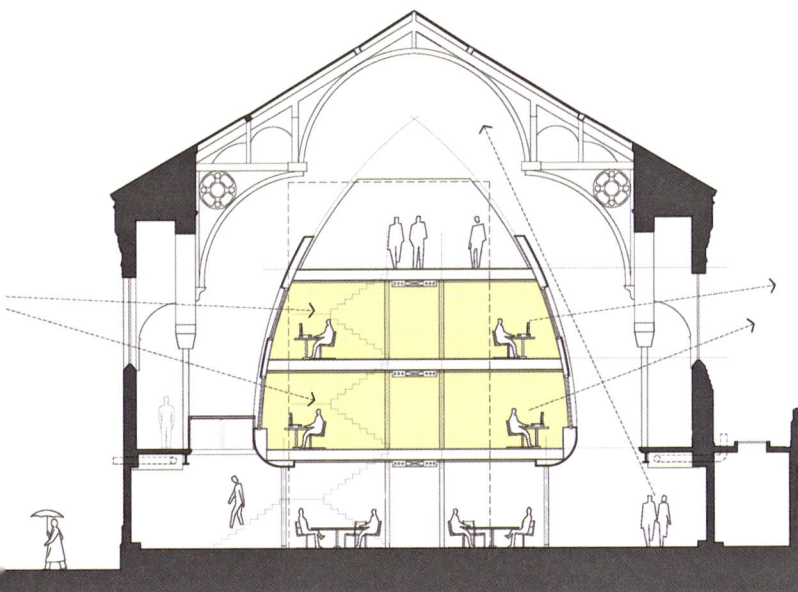

View from ground floor
Bridge connection to existing first floor gallery
The curved form allows much of existing fabric to remain visible
Cross section illustrating new structure within former main pool hall
External view from Henry Square

PETER'S HOUSE COPENHAGEN DENMARK STUDIO DAVID THULSTRUP 2015

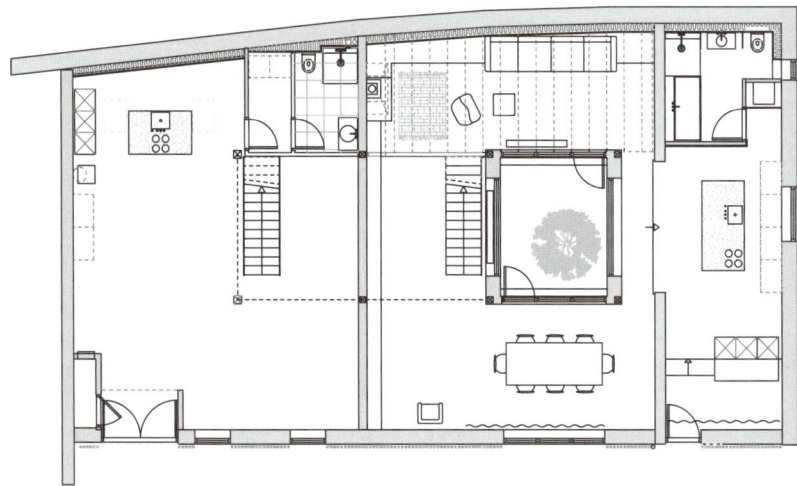

Terrace
Ground floor plan
Dining area

The guiding inspiration for photographer Peter Krasilnikoff's private residence and studio evolved from worn-out warehouses and factories. Three raw brick walls of the original garage building were retained, which in its original form enabled little natural light to flow into the interior. A glass-walled atrium in the center of the building provided the solution, allowing natural light to flood into all three floors of the residence. Specially selected greenery was planted in the atrium, which has been remodeled to form a green core.

The entire building is clad with vertical strips of Brazilian hardwood. On the ground floor, raw poured concrete contrasts with blackened steel paneling and the original raw brick walls. On the first floor the material is contrasted with light oak walls and a terrazzo-lined bathroom in a soft gray hue. A special feature is a glass-walled roof room which opens up to a richly planted terrace and was created with the particular needs and desires of Peter Krasilnikoff in mind.

NOW: THE NEW HOUSE, CREATED BY DAVID THULSTRUP, IS A CONSTRUCTIVE ARCHITECTURAL AND MATERIAL-BASED WORK. SPREAD ACROSS 500 SQUARE METERS, THE CONTRASTING BUILDING IS MAINLY REMODELED WITH CONCRETE, GLASS, OAK AND TERRAZZO.

PAST: THE OLD GARAGE BUILDING WAS BUILT IN THE 1930S. IT WAS USED AS A MECHANICS WORKSHOP GARAGE AND WAS CHARACTERIZED BY RAW-BRICK WALLS.

275
ZALANDO OUTLET – PREMIUM ZONE FRANKFURT/ MAIN GERMANY DESIGN IN ARCHITEKTUR 2015

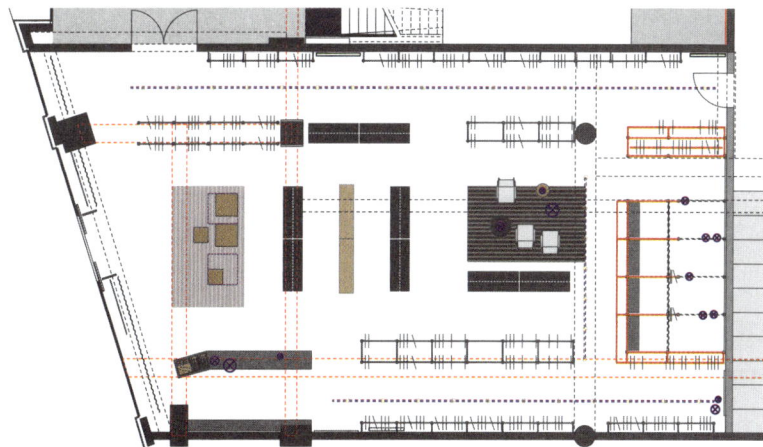

View into premium store with new counter
Compact Density Fiberboard and copper tubes
Ground floor plan
Curtains consciously cover parts of insight

The newly created Premium Zone is located on the ground level of the Zalando outlet. A heavy, silver-sheened curtain behind the glass façade largely conceals the store within. Lettering hung from copper clothes hangers and spelling out the word "Premium" and the theatrical staging of the storefront are designed to arouse the customer's curiosity.

Inside, the concrete floor was deliberately left in its raw state, while electrical cables are installed on the ceiling in full visibility. The existing zones of the outlet on the upper levels are bright in color and there is layout designed for the mass presentation of goods. In contrast, the zones on the ground floor are dominated by gray and black, combined with copper-colored surfaces. A lighting sculpture above the tables was designed specifically for this shop. Entering this minimalist yet esthetically rich store, the visitor can view the entire space, all the way to the changing rooms. The black changing rooms are framed and delineated by a construction made of copper water pipes. The payment counter is covered with a layer of copper sheeting, while the wall behind features pastel-colored Art Nouveau tiles.

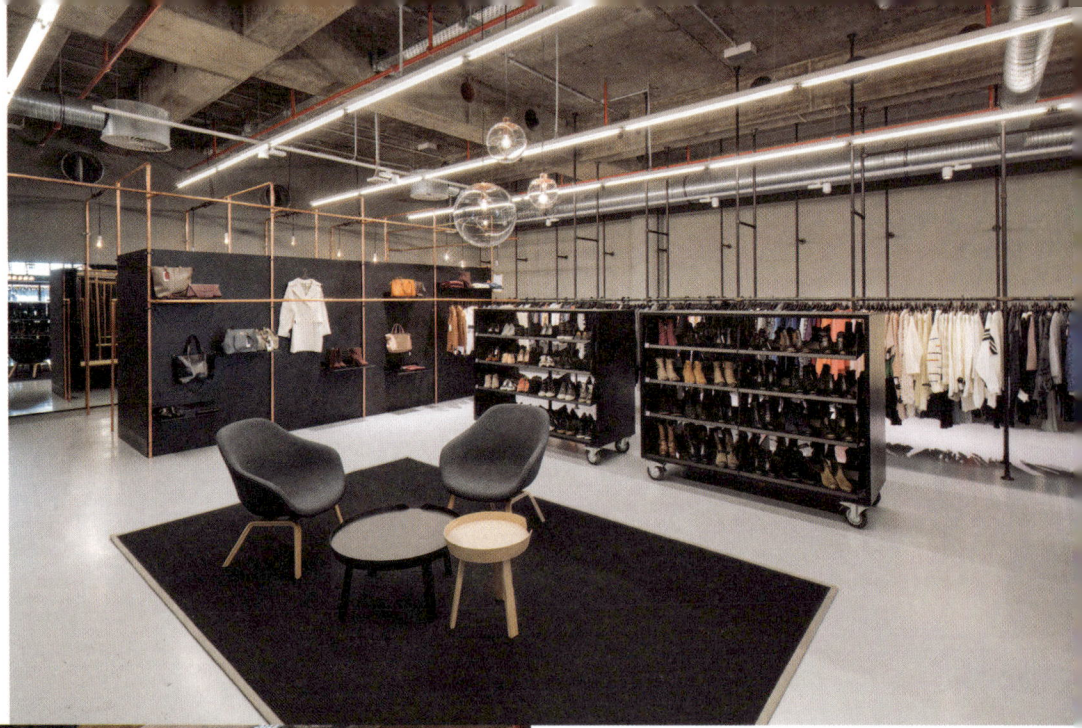

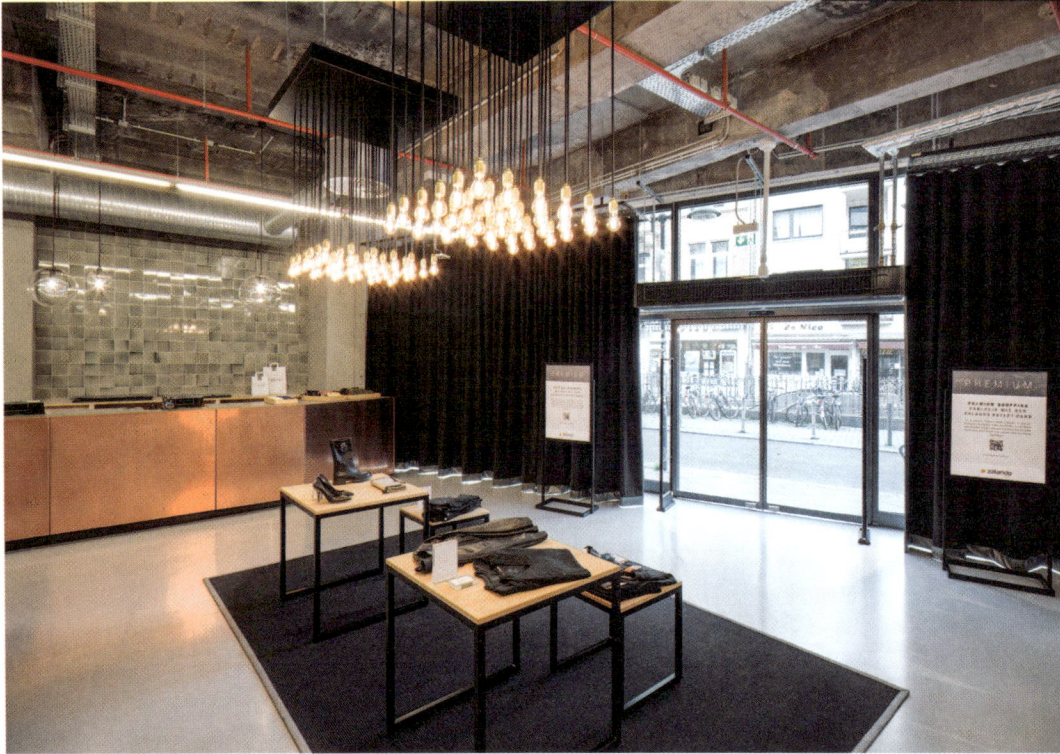

NOW: DESIGN IN ARCHITEKTUR RE-ESTABLISHED THIS HOUSE FOR ZALANDO OUTLETS AS RESIDENTIAL AND OFFICE BUILDING. SPREAD ACROSS 270 SQUARE METERS, MAINLY COPPER, COPPER TUBES, CRUDE STEEL, BLACK LACQUER, AND KRONOSWISS CDF WERE USED.

PAST: THE ORIGINAL RESIDENTIAL AND OFFICE BUILDING, A REINFORCED CONCRETE STRUCTURE WITH A NATURAL STONE FAÇADE, WAS ERECTED IN THE 1990S. APART FROM REINFORCED CONCRETE AND NATURAL STONE, GLASS WAS USED TO CONSTRUCT THE BUILDING.

Raw concrete ceiling with installations in waiting area
Copper counter and light sculptures in entrance area
Detail of copper tube
Inside changing room

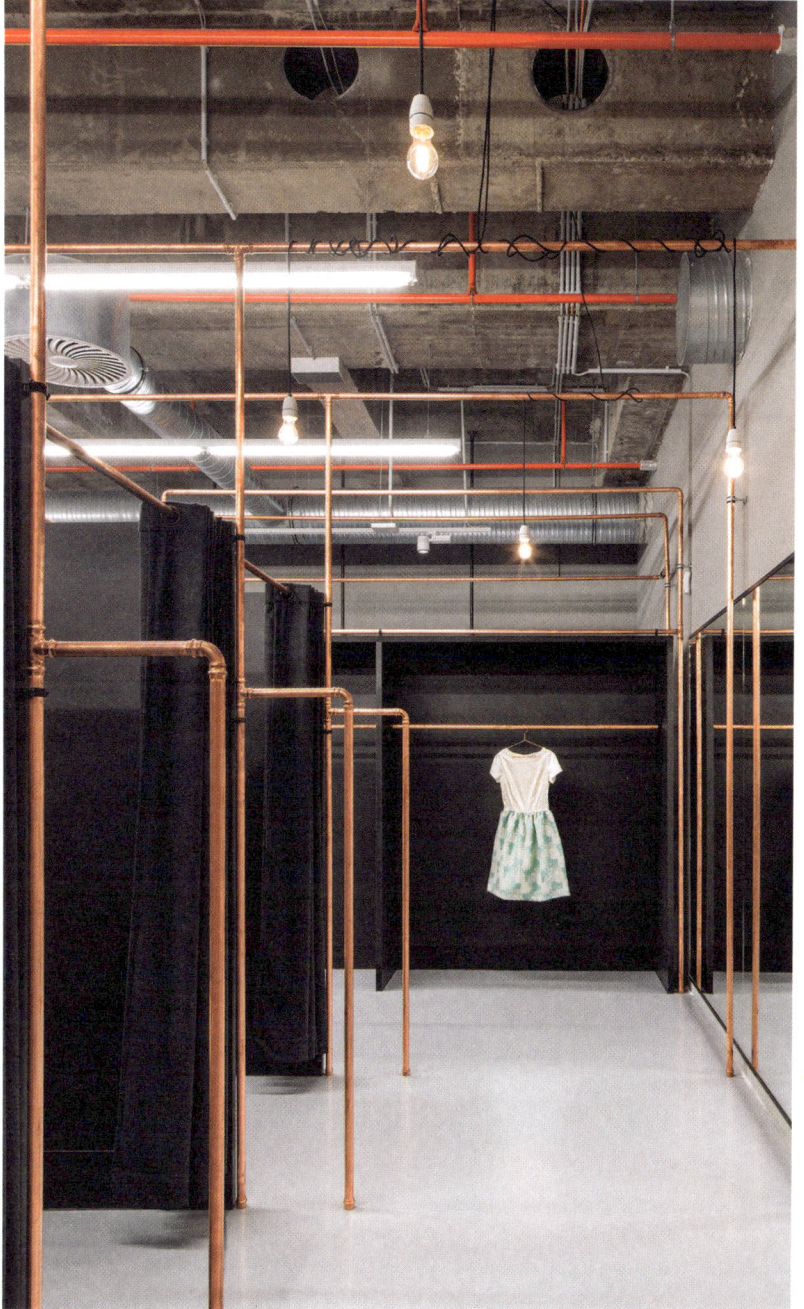

278

STORK
RESTAURANT
AMSTERDAM
THE NETHER-
LANDS
CUBE
ARCHITECTEN
SOLUZ
ARCHITECTEN
2011

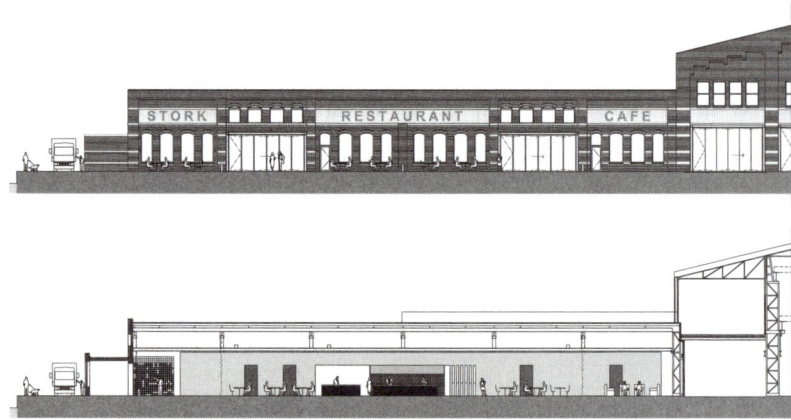

Seating area in front of restaurant
Sections of transformed warehouse
Interior with bar and different seating areas
Restaurant is often used as event location

Stork Restaurant is one of the pioneers in the project "De Overkant" where an old industrial complex of several buildings has been transformed into a lively area for creative companies, restaurants and events.

This location has the potential to become a unique and high-quality, mixed-use area in the near future. The original façades only had windows on the upper parts, so the first intervention was to create large openings with glass folding doors that can open up large parts of the façade. These interventions draw light into the old factory, create an impressive view of the harbor, and provide easy access to the waterside terrace in summertime. For much of the styling, re-used items were chosen by Interior Shock, including huge concrete sewerage segments, large old cable reels and wooden pallets. With this minimal input of new material, it was possible to create the atmosphere of a restaurant inside the vast old warehouse. A large central bar was placed between the café section and the more formal restaurant area. The open space is divided into different areas, each with their own particular atmosphere.

NOW: EIGEN HAARD COMMISSIONED CUBE ARCHITECTEN AND SOLUZ TO REDEVELOP THE 30,000 SQUARE METERS OF INDUSTRIAL SPACE OVER A PERIOD OF AT LEAST 15 YEARS. THE RESTAURANT WITH 1,100 SQUARE METERS WAS TRANSFORMED USING NEW WINDOWS AND DISTINCTIVE INTERIOR DESIGN ELEMENTS.

PAST: THE INDUSTRIAL AND OPEN CHARACTER OF THE OLD WAREHOUSE WAS THE PERFECT SPOT TO CREATE AN ATTRACTIVE CAFÉ AND THE BIGGEST FISH RESTAURANT IN EUROPE. THE BUILDING IS SITUATED ALONG THE ATTRACTIVE AMSTERDAM WATERFRONTS.

Round tables support open space character
Industrial ambience
Extraordinary lighting design
Pallets create a comfortable lounge area

MILLION DONKEY HOTEL PRATA SANNITA ITALY FELD72 ARCHITEKTEN 2006

Diagram of "flying bed"
"Flying bed" from above
"Flying bed" in context of Million Donkey Hotel

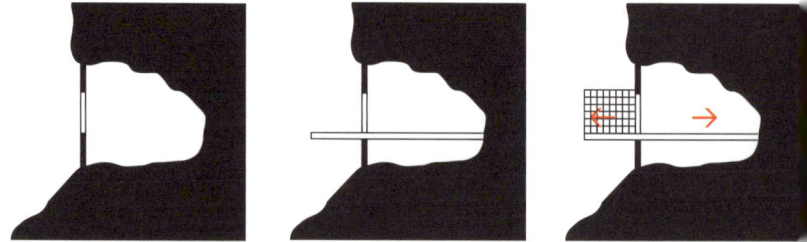

The challenge facing the architects was to create a hotel in just 24 days. The architects saw the vacant spaces in Prata Sannita, a shrinking village in southern Italy with scarcely more than 1,500 inhabitants, as rife with potential. The countless empty rooms conjured up visions of a scattered hotel. Within a month, and with the help of more than 40 volunteers from the village and a material budget of 10,000 euros, bedrooms and a special bathroom were developed and built.

One year later the process of development continued, this time with the focus on the public spaces. A stairwell with amphitheater, a terrace room and a bar were erected directly adjacent to the existing hotel rooms. In the off-season, the rooms can be used by the local residents as an extension of the public spaces. This sustainable project that uses local resources arose as the result of a series of negative circumstances; hugely benefitting the local economy. The Million Donkey Hotel is now being further developed by the organization Local Heroes.

NOW: FELD72 ARCHITEKTEN RESTRUCTURED THE ROOMS IN JUST 24 DAYS WITH THE HELP OF OVER 40 LOCAL VOLUNTEERS AND CREATED THIS SPECTACULAR HOTEL INVITED BY THE PAESESAGGIO WORKGROUP AND THE REGION CAMPANIA. LOCAL MATERIALS SUCH AS NATURAL STONE AND STEEL WERE RECYCLED AND USED FOR THE RENOVATION.

PAST: THE BUILDINGS IN THE MEDIEVAL VILLAGE ARE MAINLY CHARACTERIZED BY TUFF.

Bedroom "The Black Hole"
Bedroom "The Silver Space"
"Flying bed" in use
View from "flying bed"

V12
GALICIA
SPAIN
VENTURA ESTUDIO
2009

Former patio transformed into living room
Restored façade

V12 stands in the ruins of an old rural Galician house in the Lugo Province. All the original stonewalls and façades were kept to maintain the character of the original building. The interior was entirely renewed to create an atmosphere of luminosity and spaciousness, but only original materials such as chestnut wood for flooring and granite were used to preserve the original character.

Hidden frame windows were used to disguise the modern changes – from the outside, only the preserved stone façade is visible. The original patio, where all the animals used to be kept, was incorporated into the interior of the house. Yet the dwelling's former spaces are not hidden by the new distribution – the patio, original kitchen and storage spaces are all visible. Some large stones were left uncovered to show the original construction system, while the changes the house has experienced through its history are visible on the exterior façade. Old radiators recovered from a construction site in Madrid were incorporated as a key design element.

NOW: VENTURA ESTUDIO RE-ESTABLISHED THIS BUILDING AS A PRIVATE HOUSE. SPREAD ACROSS 400 SQUARE METERS, THE ORIGINAL DWELLING WAS TRANSFORMED BY USING GRANITE STONE, CHESTNUT WOOD AND CEMENT TO CREATE AN HARMONIOUS CONNECTION BETWEEN OLD AND NEW.

PAST: THE ORIGINAL, TRADITIONAL GALICIAN HOUSE WAS BUILT IN THE LATE NINETEENTH CENTURY. BY USING LOCAL GRANITE STONE, THE ARCHITECT CREATED A HOUSE CHARACTERIZED BY THE TYPICAL RURAL STYLE.

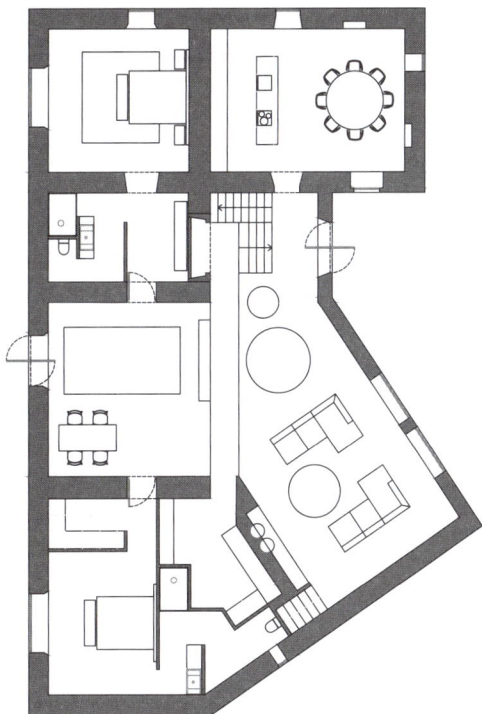

Bathroom
Living room
Kitchen
Ground floor plan
View from entrance

290

SIKMUL
SEOUL
SOUTH
KOREA
DESI_
ARCHITECTS
2015

Different chairs around table
Some of the old walls have been torn down

In the center of Seoul desi_architects, in cooperation with Louis Park, have created a new café bar. Four neglected hanoks, traditional houses in the Jongno District, were reused in this project. The renovation comprises a vivid open art space and café bar. Some of the walls were torn down in order to merge various different areas and create a single larger space.

The roof was replaced with transparent glass, and individual original roof tiles were reused to construct new walls for a unique look that preserves the warm aura of the traditional buildings. The main façade was constructed with Plexiglas. Inside, the remains of the old walls were preserved; when the interior lights are turned on, their silhouette can be seen from outside. Past and present are both projected simultaneously in this visual feature. The seating area on one side of the building is open to the street, allowing guests to enjoy an outdoor atmosphere. In this project, traditional design is preserved yet rendered fresh and innovative in a novel manifestation of the charm and beauty of traditional Korean architecture.

NOW: TO BUILD THIS CAFÉ BAR, DESI_ARCHITECTS GUTTED THE RUIN, REUSED THE ROOF-TILES TO BUILD NEW WALLS STANDING WITHIN THE OLD WALLS, AND ADDED A GLASS AND STEEL CANOPY.

PAST: THIS STRUCTURE WAS A HANOK, A TYPICAL TRADITIONAL HOUSE IN THE JONGNO DISTRICT OF SEOUL, CONSTRUCTED PRIMARILY USING WOOD AND CLAY.

New skylights
The canopy stands inside the old structure
Remaining handcrafted materials and new industrial
elements
Glass walls and courtyard

DE BAKKERS-WINKEL ROTTERDAM THE NETHER-LANDS
PIET HEIN EEK
2015

Entrance area with large chandelier
Bakery counter

In 1997 Piet Hein Eek received a commission to design and make the furniture for Piet Hekker's only Bakkerswinkel, a bakery that has since become something of an institution in the Netherlands. Over the last decade that first Bakkerswinkel has inspired the development of many more, each one made unique by its particular location, the building in which it's housed and the people who work there.

The tastes and personalities of everyone involved, from the designers to the shop staff, conspire to generate a new and different space with every iteration of the bakery. The architects of this store wanted to create a shop that was more beautiful than any of the existing branches. The new Bakkerswinkel, located in Rotterdam, no longer feels like a daytime café, but is instead more like a restaurant. All the interior features – sofas, hand-folded lamps, fencing, a copper bar, and a two-tone cupboard with interlocking shelves – were kept purposefully simple, both to ensure the project remained within budget and in rejection of the premise that beauty can only come with great expense.

NOW: PIET HEIN EEK RENOVATED THIS BUILDING FOR PIET HEKKER AS A BAKERY. SPREAD ACROSS 320 SQUARE METERS, THE FORMER BANK BUILDING IS NOW MAINLY USED FOR SELLING PASTRIES.

PAST: THE ORIGINAL BANK BUILDING WAS BUILT BY VAN DER HEYDEN AND NIEUWEN-HUYZEN FOR DIESTAR B.V. IN 1908. THE FORMER BUILDING WAS CONSTRUCTED USING MAINLY BRICK AND GRANITE.

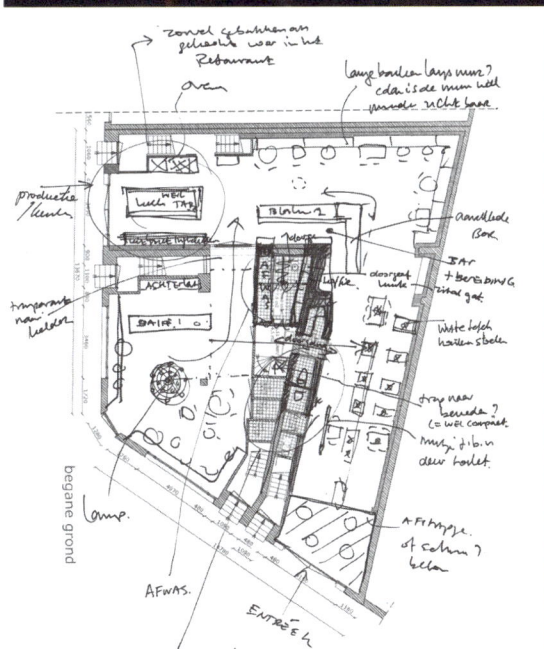

Pastry presented by bright hand-folded lamps
Seating area
Long dining table
Drawing of ground floor
Comfortable seating area with ancient armchairs

CHILDREN'S LIBRARY AND ART CENTER BEIJING CHINA ZAO/STANDARDARCHITECTURE 2014

In middle of courtyard
Section
View from above

The Cha'er Hutong courtyard situated one kilometer from Beijing's city center is a typical Da-Za-Yuan – big messy courtyard – once occupied by more than a dozen families. Over the past fifty years, each family built a small add-on kitchen in the courtyard. These annex structures are usually considered urban scrap and all of them have been removed over the last few years.

In symbiosis with the families who still live in the courtyard, a nine-square-meter community children's library, built of concrete mixed with Chinese ink, was inserted underneath the pitched roof of an existing building. One of the former kitchens was redesigned into a six-square-meter mini art exhibition space. Besides these programs, the architect also proposed classrooms for dance and painting, a local handicrafts studio, public terraces, public bathroom and other maintenance functions for the courtyard. The materials – concrete with Chinese ink and recycled gray brick – were chosen to blend in seamlessly with the surrounding urban context, while revealing warm plywood that hints at the contemporary interior within.

NOW: ZAO/STANDARDARCHITECTURE RE-ESTABLISHED THIS FORMER RESIDENCE FOR BEIJING DASHILAR - LIULICHANG CULTURAL DEVELOPMENT LTD. AS A LIBRARY AND ART CENTER FOR CHILDREN. SPREAD ACROSS 145 SQUARE METERS, IT IS NOW MAINLY USED FOR READING BOOKS AND ARTISTIC ACTIVITIES. MAIN MATERIALS INCLUDE GRAY BRICK, CONCRETE, WOOD, STEEL AND GLASS.

PAST: THE ORIGINAL BUILDING WAS ERECTED FOR LOCAL RESIDENTS, CONSTRUCTED USING MAINLY BRICK AND WOOD.

Children playing in mini art exhibition space
Dancing classroom
Library from inside
Library from outside

302
INDEX

PICTURE CREDITS

Cover front / left (from above to below):
Chris Court, Bruce Damonte
Cover front / right (from above to below):
Thomas Mayer, Jonathan Banks, Fotostudio 747
Cover back (from left to right, from above to below):
Iván Casal Nieto, Lincoln Barbour, Jamie Navarro, Julia Maria Max